SILENCE
SPEAKS

D0885206

SILENCE SPEAKS

from

the chalkboard

of

Baba Hari Dass

SRI RAMA PUBLISHING

Santa Cruz, California
revised edition
1997

© 1997 by Sri Rama Publishing

All rights reserved, including the right of reproduction in whole or in part in any form.

Editors: Karuna Ault, Shyama Friedberg

Design and Illustration: Dharani Dass

Production coordination: Karuna Ault

Frontispiece Photograph: Rodney Polden

Back Cover Photograph: Ward Mailliard

First Published: January, 1977

Revised Edition: June, 1997

10   9   8   7   6   5   4   3   2   1

ISBN 0-918100-19-4

Library of Congress Catalog Card Number 96-092500

Sri Rama Publishing is a non-profit organization founded to produce the writings of Baba Hari Dass. Profits from the sale of books and recordings are used to support our orphanage in northern India. (See page 272.)

BABA HARI DASS

TABLE OF CONTENTS

PREFACE

Baba Hari Dass is a monk who does not speak. The practice of keeping silence is called *mauna,* in Sanskrit. Its aim is less about silencing the voice and more about silencing the mind which, as we know, tends to be filled with worries, desires, and clingings. We are privileged to be touched through this book with advice and teachings of a spiritual master who, out of that silence, gives form to the unexplainable and sheds light on our daily life predicaments.

It has been our honor to revise and re-edit this beautiful book, originally published in 1977 with the same title. We have chosen a larger format, a new design, and have reorganized the material into specific categories for easier access. Several illustrations, drawn by the original artist, were added. Some of the wording has been updated, both to reflect contemporary English usage and for clarification of difficult concepts. We are most fortunate to have had the author's input in this endeavor, including several significant additions to the text.

Babaji writes: "There is an inner silence. It cannot be heard by the ears, only by the heart." This is the silence—the Source, the all-pervading stillness from which we come and to which we return. It is the wellspring of wisdom and peace, compassion and love. May the words in this book filter into the silent spaces of your heart. May they bring stillness to your mind. May they speak to the silence in your soul.

The Editors:

Karuna Ault
Shyama Friedberg

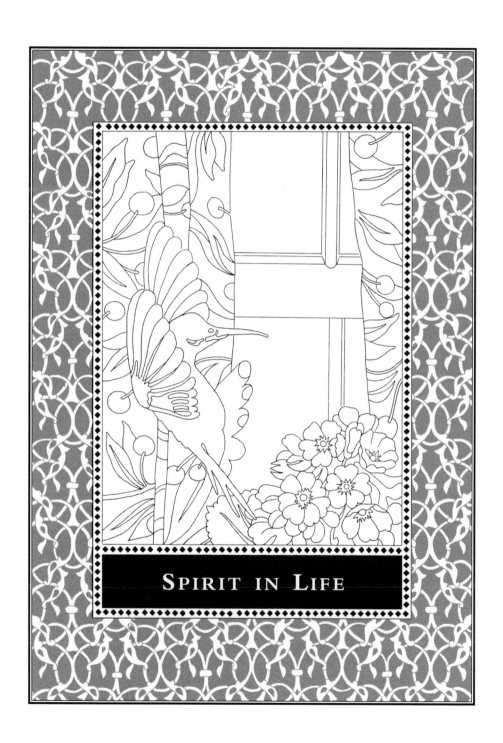

SPIRIT IN LIFE

FAITH & DEVOTION

Faith, devotion,
and right thinking are the foundation
of spirituality.
Contentment, compassion, and tolerance
are the walls. When you have built this
room for yourself you are safe
and in peace . . . God is
already with you.

What is the purpose of life? Why are we here?
To find God. To love God is our natural state.

If it's natural, why do we have to work so hard to come to it?
There is the pull of the world. Stop the pull of the world and you will see that you are in God.

Just as sweetness can't be described, in the same way love, God, enlightenment, can't be taught by words, by correspondence or by reading books. We have to start from faith and build on it until we actually can experience God.

Because we are in illusion, we give a name and form to understand God. It helps in developing faith and devotion. But if a person says that a certain form of God is the only God, then that person is in illusion within illusion. For development of faith, it can help to believe that the person's own form of God is the sole and supreme form, but no one can force others to accept a certain way. It is like a child who thinks, "My father is the strongest man in the world." For that child it is true, but it is not true for everyone.

What is the object of faith?
Faith can make God real.

Is faith also an illusion?
It is an illusion until it becomes real. Ramakrishna Paramahansa had faith in the bronze figure of Kali, and he received her grace. Actually the power was inside of him. When you meditate on an object very deeply you can realize this for yourself. The object is outside; concentrate on it. Your mind will dissolve and the curtain between inside and outside will disappear.

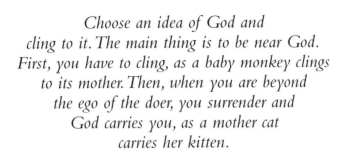

*Choose an idea of God and
cling to it. The main thing is to be near God.
First, you have to cling, as a baby monkey clings
to its mother. Then, when you are beyond
the ego of the doer, you surrender and
God carries you, as a mother cat
carries her kitten.*

Does faith transcend or invalidate the intellect?

When there is faith you don't need intellect (discrimination). You have accepted and you don't have any questions left. But you have to attain this faith. It never comes all at once. In the beginning faith and intellect work in harmony.

What is the quickest way to increase faith?

By disciplining your life pattern.

How would that increase faith?

When the life pattern is disciplined, the mind becomes more peaceful, and that peace brings faith.

Do you mean by "disciplined life" to follow some religion?

Religion can't show God. God has no religion. But it's good to follow some order or discipline.

Does it matter which order one follows?

I don't know. Some like cookies, some toast, some tea.

A path to God that disclaims other valid paths or methods is ignorance. Sometimes, when people make an idea of God and worship it with devotion they develop a kind of fanatic feeling. This creates different kinds of illusions such as disclaiming other paths, religions, sects.

How can we develop devotion?

By developing faith. It's in your hands to dance or to sit. If you feel like dancing then dance. If your aim is firm everything is yoga. In dancing you'll dance for God, in working you'll work for God, and in meditating you'll meditate for God.

Don't think
that you are carrying the whole world.
Make it easy. Make it play.
Make it a prayer.

What role does devotion play in *sadhana*?
Faith, devotion, and right thinking are three pillars of spiritual life. Devotion is the light of love. When it grows in a person it goes so deep that you can't say God and love are two different things.

In people's minds, devotion and worship are the same. Is there a difference?
Worship is the active part of devotion. In worship you do something. Devotion is a feeling of love toward God. Whether you do anything or not, still it is there.

How do I find God?
Open your heart in front of God and your prayer will be heard. A yogi searches for God in the world and says, "This is not God . . . this is not God . . . this is not God," and thereby rejects everything. As soon as God is found, the yogi says, "This is God . . . this is God . . . this is God." God is seen in everything, and everything is accepted.

*Faith and devotion
are two legs which can make us
stand and walk on the
spiritual path.*

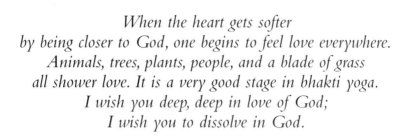

When the heart gets softer
by being closer to God, one begins to feel love everywhere.
Animals, trees, plants, people, and a blade of grass
all shower love. It is a very good stage in bhakti yoga.
I wish you deep, deep in love of God;
I wish you to dissolve in God.

What is love . . . is it real?

Lover is a form, and love is beyond that form. Lover is body, and love is soul. Love is reality. That which is experienced by lovers is not pure love because it is mixed with attachment.

God is not somewhere else; you are God.
You are God and you are in God. It's simply a matter
of acceptance. Accept yourself, accept others, and accept
the world. You will see everything is full of love,
and love is God.

Sadhana should be part of life. God is within you.
Worship God in the form of love
for all beings.

How can one develop real love, that which is above the physical plane?

To make the heart bloom, we have to stop hating others, as well as ourselves. Hate is like a frost which freezes the lake and burns the stem of the lotus flower.

Love is free from all bondage.
It cannot be created by our minds, nor can it be made
by our bodies. It exists in its own purity and shines by itself.
A lotus blooming in a lake attracts the eyes of everyone,
although it doesn't try to attract. When the lotus
of love blooms in the lake of the heart,
everyone can see it, feel it, and
then they come like bees to take its nectar.
When real love is understood, the heart will open
like a lotus when the sun rises. Let love develop
inside your heart. The purer the heart
becomes, the more love will come out, and
one day you and love will
become one.

Mount Kailasha is the abode of Lord Shiva and his
wife, Parvati. Once Shiva and Parvati were sitting on
the top of Mount Kailasha enjoying the cool air and
looking at the vast plains where there were cities,
towns, jungles, rivers. Parvati said, "My Lord, look!
Thousands of your devotees are singing in temples,
living in jungles, caves, or by the river banks
meditating on you. Why don't you give salvation to
those who are so devotional and loving?" Shiva said,
"My dear, let us go and see those devotees. Now I am
ready to give them salvation."

Shiva disguised himself as a saint and Parvati as his
disciple. They came down to the world and entered a
town. They sat in a secluded place, and if anyone came
to the saint he would tell the person's past and future.

In no time the word spread all over the adjoining towns that a high saint with powers of prophecy had arrived. Flocks of people eager to know their futures began to collect.

One day a group of devotees came who were singing and dancing, and all were intoxicated with devotion. After some chanting, one devotee, who appeared to be the leader of the group, came forward and bowed to the saint. Very meekly he said, "Guru Maharaj, will you tell me when I will get salvation? I meditate in the winter for two and one half hours, sitting in water up to my neck. During summer I meditate for two and one half hours surrounded by fires. When it rains I sit in the rain and meditate. I meditate every day for eight hours, and for several years I have been taking only a single meal of fruits and milk each day."

The saint looked at him with much surprise and said, "Oh, you are doing hard austerities! You are a very good yogi. You have much devotion." Hearing this the man felt very good and was excited to hear about his salvation. The saint continued, "If you go on doing your *sadhana* regularly, you can get salvation after three births." The devotee was shocked at hearing this. With bowed head he went back to his group saying, "Still three births!"

Another man spoke about his sadhana, and the saint told him it would be seven births. In this way everyone asked about getting salvation. The saint told one ten births, another fifteen, others twenty or thirty. Finally, when all were finished, a small, thin, man who had been hiding behind the others came forward. He was shy and afraid but he dared to say, "Sir, I don't do any sadhana, but I love God's creation, and I try not to hurt anyone by my actions, thoughts, or words. Can I get salvation?"

The saint looked at the little man and then scratched his head as if he were in some doubt. The man again bowed to the saint and nervously said, "Can I, sir?" The saint then said, "Well, if you go on loving God in the same way, maybe after a thousand births you too will get salvation."

As soon as the man heard that he could eventually get salvation, he screamed with joy, "I can get salvation! I can get salvation!" And he began to dance in ecstasy. All of a sudden his body changed into a flame. At the same time the saint and his disciple also changed into flames. All three flames merged into one and disappeared.

Shiva and Parvati were again sitting on the top of Mount Kailasha. Parvati said, "My Lord, I am very confused. You told the leader, who does such hard austerities, that he would get salvation in three births. Then you told the little man that he would get salvation in a thousand births, but you gave it to him instantly."

Shiva said, "No doubt the first devotee had much devotion and was doing austerities sincerely, but he still had an ego about his sadhana. He had not surrendered his ego yet, and three births appeared a very long time to him. The other man had so much faith that even a thousand births were very short for him. He completely surrendered to me. I did not give him salvation; it was his own faith in my words. His emotions increased so much that he could not keep the body any longer. His essence of life, the Self, took abode in me."

SPIRITUAL PRACTICE

Once a blind woman was coming
from a well at night with a pitcher of water on
her head and a lighted lantern in her hand.
A man met her on the way and said,
"How stupid! You are blind,
so why carry a lantern?" The blind woman said,
"It is so that you will not knock me down."
Our sadhana is a lantern that lights our way
and keeps us on the path
even if we're blind.

Spirituality is not simply doing *asanas, pranayama,* meditation, or singing spiritual songs. Developing good qualities within is spirituality. No one can develop these qualities in one day. An aspirant fights a constant inner battle to overpower the opposites—good and bad, pleasure and pain. In Hinduism all these things are explained in the form of stories, like the *Ramayana* and the *Mahabharata.* The wars in these stories are going on inside every human being all the time in the form of negative and positive qualities. To be aware that you are fighting these battles is sadhana, spiritual practice.

What's the point of sadhana?
To get out of the illusion of the world.

A person works hard to achieve worldly things because they are seen as real. But very few can think about the reality of the Self and work hard for it. Of those who think about it, very few can believe in it. Of those who believe, very few are free from doubts.

Would you define sadhana as spiritual practice?
Yes. Sadhana is to get perfection. What is perfection? Perfection for each person is different. You draw a line and it is perfect for you, but an artist doesn't see it as perfect. The artist draws another line and sees it as perfect. A person with a magnifying glass comes and sees the line thick and thin and says it is not perfect. The edge of a sword is so perfect, and no one can deny it, but if you see the edge under a microscope you will see that it is like a chain of mountains. Perfection has levels of subtlety.

What should I work on most in my sadhana?
Not to lean on others.

If the aim is perfect the chain of sadhana never breaks. Traveling, working, eating, talking—everything becomes sadhana.

I seem to be losing faith. Nothing significant appears to be happening to me. I keep on expecting some kind of profoundly moving, absorbing experience or transformation of my consciousness.

As long as the mind is in confusion of thoughts, nothing happens very fast. But as soon as the thought waves are stopped it happens—just as one spark can burn a huge pile of hay in one second. Regular practice purifies the mind, and an aspirant automatically adopts good qualities, which strengthens faith. There is no medicine or yoga by which a person becomes enlightened in a day.

Regular sadhana works inside the body and mind very slowly. For three or four years we actually don't understand what is happening. After that the mind gets the ability to understand the effect of sadhana. One should not be disheartened by apparent lack of progress in sadhana. There is always progress but we can't feel it, just as when an airplane is high in the sky and going very fast we can't feel its speed. The progress is felt at takeoff and landing.

We have to live in this world. The world is full of pain—even the pleasure of the world is pain. But we have to go through this pain to get bliss. Bliss is freedom from thoughts, and the world is a bundle of thoughts. By regular yoga practice, faith and devotion, and by cultivating good qualities we can attain that blissful stage. No one can give this stage to anyone. We all have to attain it by ourselves.

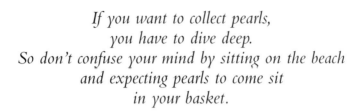

If you want to collect pearls,
you have to dive deep.
So don't confuse your mind by sitting on the beach
and expecting pearls to come sit
in your basket.

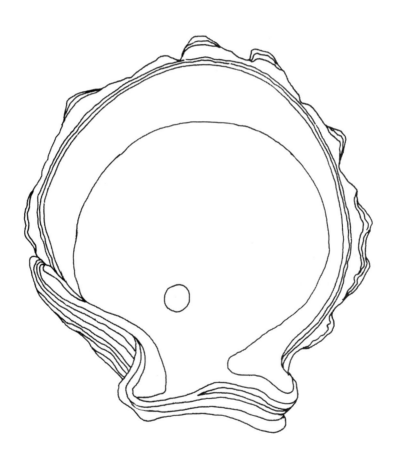

A human being has a discriminative mind, so we are capable of stopping the pull of bad tendencies. If *samskaras,* or fate, were the sole master of our lives we would not try to attain the truth. We would leave it in the hands of fate. But we don't do that. We look for food when we're hungry; we defend ourselves when attacked. We know we can't sit like a rock waiting for fate to feed and protect us, to arrange everything for our future. Since we know that fate is not our master in day to day life, in the same way we should realize we can't wait for fate to lead us to the truth. We should start working to attain the truth.

People who say, "I don't want to do anything, I just want to be," are deluded and don't know themselves. If they mean they want to sit in ignorance and pain, they will remain sitting forever.

In yoga sadhana, happiness and sadness both come. Both are part of sadhana. Without one, the other can't be experienced. But we shouldn't let them stop our practices.

I find it hard to meditate because someone is practicing on drums in the next room.
I understand how difficult it is to do sadhana while someone is beating drums next to your ears. But it is a test. It's also a sadhana inside a sadhana. If everything goes easily you can't test yourself and you can't understand where you are. Go forward slowly and firmly. Every step in sadhana should be firm so that it will not slip.

Some students are drawn to dhyana yoga, some to laya yoga, some to nada yoga, some to kundalini yoga, some to bhakti yoga, and so on.

Yoga	Characteristics
Bhakti Yoga	path of devotion
Dhyana Yoga	meditation practices
Hatha Yoga	purification of body, mastery of breath
Jñana Yoga	discrimination is cultivated through intellectual processes
Karma Yoga	selfless action
Kundalini Yoga	system of *chakras* and subtle energies
Laya Yoga	dissolving the mind into *samadhi* by means of inner sound *(nada)*, devotion *(bhakti)*, and psychic energies *(tantra)*
Mantra Yoga	power of sound vibration; includes nada yoga
Raja Yoga	also called ashtanga yoga— to distinguish between real and unreal; includes bhakti yoga
Tantra Yoga	transcendence by overcoming the bonds of the senses

A yogi should select a particular pattern of sadhana and work on it every day. Then that sadhana can be perfected. All sadhanas are for making the mind free from *vrittis* (thought waves), so what's the use of doing one thousand different things? It's not necessary to do all six purification methods, eight *pranayamas* (breath control), twenty-five *mudras**, and eighty-four *asanas* (postures). One should select things according to one's nature, or as one's teacher suggests.

Will we know our path when we start on it?
When we are determined to find it, the right path comes from inside. First thing is firm determination. We can't learn from others if we have no ability to learn. What we are learning is already inside of us; we are not getting it from outside. A person who has a musical ear can pick up music from hearing other people play. I don't mean that a teacher is not necessary, but that the quality of learning is within the student. Truth is beyond this. You can't see truth in a teacher while you are still in illusion. You have to go beyond this, and that you can do by yourself. Then there is no you and I. You and I are only an illusion.

Can one follow two different paths at once?
One path is enough to reach the destination. To go halfway by one path and then halfway by another path will not bring any progress. But if one path doesn't suit you, then you have to change it.

---

* Mudra means "seal" or "lock." Mudras are postures or gestures practiced to awaken and direct kundalini upward.

Doesn't bhakti yoga encourage a feeling of dualism? How can we be one with God?

Bhakti yoga can't be practiced without dualism—lover and beloved. In bhakti yoga an aspirant relates to God with different attitudes such as being a servant, a friend, a wife, a lover, or a parent. In higher stages the dualism remains only as labels, like sun and rays, or ocean and waves, which are not actually separate.

*Dualism is more than one
and less than two.*

A farmer had several cows and bulls. He plowed his fields using a hand plow pulled by his bulls. One day he saw that a young bull was becoming very strong. He patted it on the back and said to himself, "Tomorrow I'll put this young bull on my plow." The farmer went into his house, and the young bull was so happy he began jumping up and down. The other cows and bulls asked him what was the matter. "Tomorrow I'm going to plow," he said, filled with pride. All the younger bulls looked at him with respect as if he were becoming a king, but the old bulls just nodded and went back to their grass. The young bull was so happy that he would go up to everyone he saw and say, "Tomorrow I'm going to plow!" The next morning the farmer took him out to the field and put him under the plow. He was young and strong, so he ran very fast. All day he ran with the plow. By evening he was so exhausted he could hardly walk up to the cow shed. When he reached the shed the younger bulls all ran up to him as if he were a great warrior, and some older bulls came up and asked, "What did you do?" He looked at them and sighed, "I plowed the whole field!" And then he collapsed on the ground. The older bulls laughed and said, "In the future, go slow, don't run."

I wrote this story for you. I did the same thing as you are doing when I was about nineteen years old. I would jump like a new horse all the time, trying different methods of yoga. But I learned by experience that sadhana should go very smoothly. Some day you will also experience the same thing. If you pour too much *ghee* (clarified butter) on a fire all at once it will put out the fire. If you pour the ghee on little by little it will increase the fire. Do sadhana according to the time you can spare for it. Don't do too much and don't do too little. The main thing is to avoid the low point where the body and mind develop sloth and laziness, and also to avoid the peak point where the body and mind break from pushing too hard.

What is *atma vichara?*

"Who am I?" *(atma vichara)* is a very important question in yoga sadhana. It opens the mind and tells you why you are doing yoga. Otherwise yoga can become a mechanical process. Practicing atma vichara with yoga sadhana awakens the consciousness very quickly, but it needs truthfulness in your own mind. It is a solitary path. The way of atma vichara is so narrow that two can't be together there. It's not like bhakti yoga. The path of bhakti yoga is very wide; several can go together. The end of both paths is God.

What is the answer to the question, "Who am I?"

For this we have to search. On the gross level the answer is different for each individual, but in the end it is the same. First we search on a low level—body, friends, surroundings, and so forth—and then we see, "I am not this." In this way the search goes on and on. When the consciousness reaches the mental level it shows us a partial answer, which is not yet perfect. We understand a little, and that little again is different for each person. But when the answer comes from beyond the mental level, from the superconsciousness, then that is the perfect answer, and it is the same for everyone.

Atma vichara, "Who am I?" begins in illusion because an aspirant can't understand the subtle level of "I." But when one's consciousness becomes clearer by yoga sadhana, then one can do real atma vichara. Self-inquiry starts with words—the mind talks to itself: "I am not this, I am not this," and so on. But after regular practice it doesn't talk, it experiences: "I am not this, I am not this." This experience is the real Self-inquiry.

By running away
from the world no one can get peace.
Anywhere you go the problems will go with you,
because the problems are inside you and
not outside. Outside is simply
a projection of inside.

By doing regular sadhana the path of energy going up becomes clearer. Day by day an aspirant gains the ability to understand the difference between truth and illusion.

Can one know reality, or truth?

Truth is beyond senses. All that we experience by our senses is still illusion. But when God shines in the form of Self inside a person, association with such a person *(satsang)* makes a feeling of God, truth, love.

You have said that satsang is meeting with people who are seeking God. How can we find God outside with other people? Don't we have to meet God inside?

What is outside? Outside is a projection of inside. If we are not inside of you, then we are not outside either.

Satsang teaches us how to live together and how to love each other. This is the foundation of yoga and it is the first thing we must learn. Yoga methods are easy to learn, but learning tolerance, compassion, and contentment is difficult. We can't learn by hiding in a cave; we learn by being with people. If you float in love, then all who are around you will float in love. By sadhana one can attain this state.

Is God here, now?

It is true that God is present wherever worshipped. That's why satsang is very important. We should do more than just listen to the thoughts and ideas discussed in satsang; we must make those ideas a part of our lives. We have to take on those good qualities— otherwise we will be just like parrots who can sing mantras but don't get any benefit from them.

Life is not a burden.
We make it a burden by confusing ourselves,
by thinking about the past and making plans for the
future, and not thinking of the present.

You are in the mountains
where there is fresh air and water,
where there are trees and plants and streams.
Sit with them and enjoy the creation of God.
God and creation are not
separate.

The idea is to attain peace.

When you are working on the inside, is it proper to work spiritually on the outside also?
You don't need to work on the outside; your light will spread outside by itself.

*No one can make heaven on
earth until one has made heaven inside first.
It is like holding a candle in the dark
which is not lit and telling others,
"Follow me."*

Is there a conflict between serving humankind and serving spiritual needs?
Pranayama and holding breath isn't the only way. Everyday life should be pure and full of good qualities; then there is no conflict. A person who is aware of developing positive qualities is a real yogi. Sainthood is not in dressing in a particular dress, in giving speeches on spirituality. It's in our actions, in our behavior, in our truthfulness. Saints and non-saints are physically the same, but mentally they are different.

Is any occupation more conducive to sadhana than another, such as a farmer as opposed to a taxi cab driver, etc.?
If one has work in which one is not dependent on others, it is better for sadhana.

When I was twenty-two I lost the sight in one eye. I wonder if this affects my inner vision?
No. The inner vision is never affected even if the physical eyes get some defect.

I listen better with my eyes closed.
Because you have fear, you close your eyes when someone talks to you.

Can a person be spiritual without being a member of any spiritual group?
Although a person has no trademark of spirituality, it doesn't mean the person is unspiritual. One who is honest, truthful, loving, ready to help others, and who has less anger, pride, and jealousy is already spiritual even though not a disciple of a guru or a member of a community, sect, or *ashram*.* Yes, there are many spiritual people who never classify themselves as spiritual. This egoless spirituality is wonderful.

For a real truth seeker, to live in an ashram for the whole life is like growing plants under a huge tree. Under the shade of a big tree the plant first grows, then its growth stops. One should practice yoga independently, taking full responsibility for oneself. Group discipline is only to maintain a group. In yoga, only self-discipline is important. An army is very disciplined, but they don't get enlightenment. When you are in a group you have to accept the discipline of the group, not because the discipline will give you enlightenment, but to make the work of the group easier. In a group doing the same kind of sadhana, all individuals will not attain the same results, because each is different in gross body, subtle body, and in samskaras. A group or ashram is good only for learning. When you have learned everything, you have to practice by yourself.

---

* Ashram is a home, living quarters, for a group of people who have similar spiritual goals.

Living in a community is a different thing. The aim is to fulfill a desire to live in a joint family. This is a natural desire in human beings and in certain animals. Because in western culture there is no joint family system, the natural desire comes out in a different way. Your sadhana is your own personal thing and not a part of the community. The methods are for achieving purity and clarity of mind so as to be able to distinguish between truth and illusion. To watch yourself every moment is yoga. To attain the ability of watching yourself, you practice all the other methods—asana, pranayama, meditation, and so on.

All aspirants want to become like Jesus, Buddha,
or other famous saints;
but they don't want to face the hardships
Jesus and Buddha faced.

MANDALAS, MANTRA, MAUNA

We have to trick

the mind by various methods

to prevent it from forming thoughts.

You will learn

by your own higher stage

of consciousness.

I'd like to ask about *mandalas*. In order to reach desired results, does a person pick a certain mandala and then change it from time to time?
Mandalas are designed to invoke certain energies. A method of worship using *mantras* and mandalas is tantra.

What are mandalas?
Mandalas are energy instruments, and the movements of planets work on mandalas. There is the dot, which is the *bindu,* or energy center; the triangle, which represents the three energies, or *gunas;* the square which represents the four minds; and the circle, which represents infinity. These things are put together in various ways, and they can be read.

If one makes a mandala, one's own mandala, is it a good thing to concentrate on?
Concentration is always good. Do it any way you can.

What is the benefit of using mandalas?
Mandala is a tantric language, a way of explaining energy. If you meditate on a mandala with its meaning it can help concentration.

Does every mandala have one meaning?
Each line, circle, triangle, square, color has a meaning.

Are there some that heal?
Yes.

What is the power in mantra?
Mantra* is sound, which activates the energy centers. In the beginning there was sound—no earth nor life. There was nothing but bliss. Then creative energy overpowered it, and the sound became bindu—a point of energy. It split in two and assumed a form like a figure eight—consciousness plus energy. From this the whole universe took form. Eventually ignorance overpowered creative energy, and desires and attachments were born to sustain the world.

Why don't you speak?
One reason is to avoid quarrels. The second is because talking causes loss of energy. Energy is lost primarily in two ways—by sex and by talking. The origin of both sound and sex is *muladhara chakra* at the base of the spine. When we talk we do so by exhalation, and we use tremendous energy this way. This can be felt if you

---

* A syllable, word, or phrase repeated in meditation.

stop talking for a few days and then start talking again. By not talking we preserve energy which can be used for meditation.

Are mantras and *kirtan* (call-and-response chanting) okay while in *mauna* (silence)?
If you can do complete silence that is better. If you do mantra and *kirtan* while in *mauna* that is okay.

What is silence?
No thoughts. Silencing the mind is real silence. To stop talking is one way to begin to silence the mind.

Silence is an austerity. You control your desire to talk. By talking, people try to impress others and attract others, which you can't do if you are in silence. In silence you have to develop tolerance. At first it is difficult to do because you separate yourself from others by not expressing yourself. But gradually the mind reduces that ego, which develops acceptance, tolerance, and reduces anger.

I have a real yearning to be silent for a while, but I have a family and a job and don't know how to do it.
I have a larger family *[indicating the gathering of devotees]*. You can do it when you get time.

I guess I am embarrassed to do it in public.
Anything is easy if you want to do it.

As long as the mind is filled with *vrittis* (thought waves) one can't see who one really is. Inner silence (stopping of vrittis) is the only way by which we can see the real Self.

MIND/INTELLECT

*You are in bondage
by your own consciousness and
you can be free by your own consciousness.
It's only a matter of turning the angle
of the mind.*

The body is like a chariot made of eight substances: blood, skin, flesh, fat, bones, marrow, semen, and aura. This chariot is pulled by two strong horses, mental energy and *pranic* energy, which are mutually dependent. Mental energy is fed by pranic energy; but without the mind, *prana* (life force) could not reach its goal, which is attainment of God. Mental energy has four functions: mind *(manas),* the recording faculty which receives impressions gathered by the senses from the outside world; intellect *(buddhi),* the discerning faculty which makes judgments and separates the real from the unreal; ego *(ahamkara),* the faculty of identification, both with the world of objects and with God, consciousness *(chitta),* the generalized field in which the other three mental faculties merge and work together. We can't ignore the mind in yoga because it is the instrument by which higher consciousness is attained.

*Anything that is accepted by the mind
comes into existence, and when it is rejected by the mind
its existence disappears. The world is just like a dream
that is created by the mind and is experienced as real
until we awaken; then it disappears.*

The mind and the five senses are for examination, discrimination, and identification with the world. They are the traps in life that keep a person in illusion. But without the mind and senses, peace can't be attained. An average person sees immediate gain—sensual pleasure—and can't ever see beyond, where there is peace.

What does intellect (buddhi) do that mind (manas) doesn't?

Mind (manas) functions within the senses; the intellect (buddhi) functions above the senses. For example, when you see an airplane crash, it is the mind that processes what the eyes, ears, nose bring to it. The intellect then judges that it was a tragic event. The ego (ahamkara) identifies with the pain of the people in the crash.

When we get to a higher level, beyond senses, do we perceive differently?

Then we perceive reality, which is quite different from the world.

Can past and future be perceived outside of senses, outside of time?

Past, present, and future are perceptions on a gross level.

How is the discriminative function (buddhi) altered when one attains liberation?

The mind assumes its *sattvic* form and discrimination is on a higher level. For instance, one doesn't see a person's color, caste, or country. Discrimination between real and unreal is what counts.

What is unreal?

The world.

Some schools say we become what our minds dwell upon.

Yes, it's true. A yogi sings "*aham Brahman* (I am God)," all the time, and the mind concentrates on it so deeply that the yogi begins to feel that he or she is God.

Everything is in you, and you project it outside. You see what you want to see.

Do higher minds guide us like intermediaries between ordinary mind and God?

Higher mind is consciousness. It has several stages. It guides us all the way up to God.

How do you feel about acts of discriminative wisdom which distance one from others?

As long as this distance is there, it is not real discriminative wisdom. You are associating discriminative wisdom with the gross world; it is beyond that. It comes when a person gets dispassion from the world. Ramakrishna Paramahansa, Ramana Maharshi, Chaitanya Mahaprabhu, Buddha, Krishna, Rama, and all incarnations of other religions took birth, did their worldly duties, and lived in society. Their discriminative wisdom did not distance them from others.

We are always judging things. What is the difference between judging and discrimination?

Do you judge, or compare, or discriminate? Judgment is the action of comparison plus discrimination. This is all on the worldly plane. Discrimination between reality and illusion is a function of higher consciousness, which comes when a person attains superconsciousness (samadhi). Then there is no question of judging.

In regard to discrimination, I always feel guilty for not having done everything right.

You are speaking about worldly discrimination. For that a person needs a clear mind. Even then we each see everything differently, according to our own point of view.

The Self is God and the world is a
projection of your mind.

Knowledge can't be taught.
It is attained by sadhana (spiritual practice).
The knowledge that can be explained by words
is not real knowledge. It is like explaining sweetness,
which you can't understand without tasting.
If you taste sweetness, you don't
need words to understand it.

What is mind?
A heap of thoughts.

How can I discriminate between imagination and intuition?
Only by a purified mind. Intuitive knowledge comes through purity of mind, developed by deep meditation. It is not guided by desires; it is a flash of higher consciousness. If the mind is involved in worldly affairs this energy is dissipated.

Is there such a thing as omniscience? Is there anyone who is all-knowing, all-seeing?
It is the stage of *parama siddha*—one who can see the world as if it were an apple on the palm. If there were no such thing there wouldn't be a word for it.

How is the world created? The world is created by our own mind. By our mind it is expanding. By our mind its reality exists. Each person's world is that person's own mind. Just as we can't dream anyone else's dream, so we can't see the world of another. But we all exist in the worlds of each other.

So our imagination manifests as this world?
It manifests in one sense. If you think of Mount
Everest, it manifests in your mind.

Is it the truth that everything is meaningless?
Simply saying that is meaningless. If you really believe
it, it is another thing—it is a method of dispassion.
When illusion *(maya)* is gone there is truth. Maya is a
veil over truth.

Does an enlightened person see the veils?
One cannot see another's maya or world, as one
cannot dream another's dream.

**If the universe is illusory, what is the knowledge
gained by scientific methods?**
There are three kinds of knowledge: *jñana, vijñana,* and
ajñana. Jñana is knowledge of the subtle elements,
vijñana is scientific knowledge of the elements, ajñana
is wrong knowledge, or ignorance. Scientific
knowledge is real as long as we relate to the world as
real; it is illusion if we understand the world is a
projection of our minds.

**What does that mean, "the world is a projection
of the mind"?**
We see what we want to see. If we don't want to see
something, we don't see it. This "want" creates the
form of the object outside. But there is an object
minus the "want" of the seer, which is reality. One
who sees that reality is called an enlightened being.

Sages say that learning is of no use, so why do it?
Anything you learn by the senses and mind is
ignorance. Real knowledge can only be obtained by
higher consciousness.

How does one change intellectualizing into real knowledge?
The only way is to concentrate and make the mind able to understand reality. By yoga you can change the intellectual knowledge of the gross body into knowledge of the subtle body. So the first thing is to practice meditation. A child has intellectual knowledge, but it is different from that of an adult. There is a similar difference between the intellectual knowledge of an ordinary person and a yogi. From books you can understand only so much, like seeing a picture of a fire—you can understand it is fire, but it can't burn your hand. A picture of a lion can show you what a lion looks like, but you can't feel the reality of the lion. Real understanding comes by experiencing.

Your questions can't go beyond
intellectual understanding, and one who goes
beyond intellectual understanding
can't question.

The world itself is a question and its answer is inside us. By study, reading, or travel we will learn something, but we cannot get complete knowledge. We can get this only by concentrating deeply inside. When the mind is free from thoughts we can see what we really are. We can discriminate real from unreal.

Is there a point where there is no discrimination at all?
When complete truth is obtained, there is only God.

A bird flies into a room and can't get out.
She flies all over the room seeking a way out, and
when she can't find a way, she gets tired and simply sits
in one corner. Then someone opens the door and takes the
bird out. We fly around in the room of the mind, and
when we realize that there is no way to get out,
we sit peacefully and wait for God
to free us.

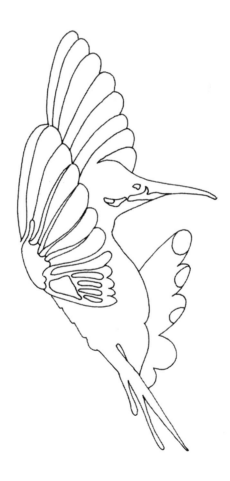

To control the mind is the most difficult job in the world. So it needs much practice. Go on doing regular sadhana. Once the mind is hooked it can't run away. The mind revolts when it is disciplined or when its out-going thought waves (vrittis) are blocked. That's why some renunciates *(sadhus)* do hard austerity *(tapas)*. But if you understand the mind's nature, then gradually it calms down.

Mind always seeks comfort. When a little hardship comes, your mind thinks of the old days when you lived with your parents and were without any responsibilities. But time always changes. You can't ever go back and be the same. The heaviest burden in life is to carry on with your responsibilities. Without this, you can't grow. You are afraid of getting nothing from your hard work. If you do your work as a duty and leave the result to God, then you will not be afraid, upset, and depressed.

The mind always makes so much trouble in meditation. Instead of fighting it, can I make it my friend and ask it to come along and enjoy the peace?
It's very difficult to control the mind. It is said, "A mustard seed can stay on a bull's horn more easily than the mind can stay on one object." It means it is very difficult, but not impossible.

When people see thoughts on a subtle plane, do these thoughts have form?
Thoughts are given form by the mind.

I see thoughts like spirals.
In you, it's true. Some feel thoughts like tangled barbed wire.

You should not be afraid of your mind.
It revolts in every person in the beginning of yoga practice.
The mind is like a wild horse that doesn't want anyone to
sit on its back. When one tries to tame it, it jumps more.
If you don't tame it, it will not jump; but it cannot
be used for uplifting the consciousness.
So taming is very important.
One should not put too much pressure on the mind
in taming it. Try to understand the mind peacefully.
Just as a horse trainer feeds and pats the horse—slowly,
carefully, and peacefully—so you can tame the mind.
Living in jungles, fasting, and doing hard austerities is also
a way, but it is dangerous and creates much pain.
You should choose a middle path.
Don't let the mind be scattered and don't put too
much pressure on it. You will see that
slowly it will change.

Virtue and vice, pleasure and pain, all are mental states that affect us only when we identify ourselves with the mind and think of ourselves as doers and enjoyers.

Can intellect aid understanding?
It helps in the beginning, but cannot give full enlightenment. The mind is the main instrument to gain enlightenment, but enlightenment is only reached when the mind stops.

How can we stop the mind?
Not by hitting it with a hammer. Stop the mind by the mind.

*It's good that you
can see your mind going to other objects
and forgetting yoga and your aim. You can pull
your mind in again when you are aware of it.
The mind is made of subjects and objects,
and it's the nature of the mind
to jump like a monkey from
one tree to another.*

Ninety percent of everyone's mind is in confusion. We don't see, taste, or smell ninety percent of what we could experience. Everything happens in confusion by reflex action. Because we have repeated the same things over and over again for several lifetimes, ninety percent of the action in our bodies is reflex action. When we understand this confusion and try to really hear, see, and taste—then we can feel the difference.

POWERS

Once Ramakrishna Paramahansa said,
"Why cross a river by using siddhis
(supernatural powers) when we can
cross it by paying one cent
to a boatman?"

A man once did sadhana
in a jungle cave. God gave him darshan
(audience) and asked, "What would you like?"
"That whatever I think will come true," he replied.
"All right. Anything you think will be true."
The man became very happy.
He thought of good food, and the food was there.
He thought about a nice bed, and the bed
was there. All of a sudden he thought,
"What will happen if this cave falls down?"
As soon as he thought this,
the cave fell down.

He got power,
but he had no control over his mind
because his sadhana was not deep enough.
We need to do sadhana so that we will become able
to control our thoughts. Only then will we
be able to benefit from the powers
that can come with higher
consciousness.

How does one explain the psychic abilities of some people, like Uri Geller?

Some are born with that talent, just as some poets, musicians, painters, scientists are born with their talents. Some develop powers by regular practice of yoga methods.

That should not be our goal?

In animals there are such powers by nature. A human being has all animal powers. They are in everyone. All we have to do is open up to what is already in us. But attaining powers and attaining the truth are two different things. If truth is realized, then there is no need for any powers.

I know a doctor who has a fifteen-year-old son who has certain psychic powers, like Uri Geller. They wonder if those powers could be used to heal people.

The boy has the state of *bhava pratyaya,* which means "born with powers," as some are born musicians or poets.

Can he turn it into something useful, for healing?

The healer needs purity of mind. If the mind is pure, one can heal sicknesses. In India there are three methods of healing: tantra, which works by exciting the emotions; mantra, which works through the chanting of sacred words or sounds; and *yantra,* which works through geometric forms, colors, diagrams, herbs, and medicines.

Why do so few yogis demonstrate the healing powers they supposedly have?

If yogis show their powers, people will follow them all

the time, and bring money, fame, and attachment. For a yogi, these can be distractions on the spiritual path. That is why it is said that demonstrating powers can be a trap.

When a saint appears in two different places at the same time, what does the saint experience?
Both forms can function differently. The awareness is the same.

If one body was here and one body in Mexico, would only one of the bodies remember?
Both bodies will remember each other. They are not two, but two puppets controlled by one puppeteer—two bodies, one consciousness.

It seems that realization of the truth behind powers can enlighten the mind.
Enlightenment and realization of the truth are the same. A person who has powers can remain unenlightened.

DREAMS

To dream of chakras,
light, fire, water, wind, and the elements
of your own body is an indication
of purified nerve channels.
To dream of the thousand-petaled lotus
is very good. Learn to control
your dreams.

Dream is caused by desires, imagination, and memory.

Dream is a function of the subtle body. When the physical body sleeps, the subtle body takes over. It recollects actions and thoughts, and produces visions of them in the mind. Usually there is no mental control over dreams; the pictures flow in a confusing and disorderly fashion. Through sadhana one can learn to control one's dreams. By so doing one may overcome samskaras, the very factor that causes rebirth. One may achieve partial or even total enlightenment in dreams by willing to do so.

What are our dreams?
Our actions of present, past, and far past are in the subconscious. When the physical body sleeps, these impressions rotate, and they feel real to our senses.

What are the dreams rotating around?
The mind is always active, even in our sleep. All impressions rotate in the mind. If you watch dreams you find they make a strange story; some parts come from different events in the present and past, and some come from past lives. One who learns to watch dreams can read the past and see the future.

What is the difference between astral projections and dreams?
A vast difference. When we dream we cannot control the dream; if we could it would be astral projection.

Are there emotions and ego in astral projection?
Without ego nothing can be projected. Emotions are also there in their subtle form. When we fly in our astral body and meet someone, we can feel the pain and emotions of that person.

I know several people who say astral travel can be helpful on the spiritual path. Is this true?
If they are really doing it.

Dream, astral travel, and samadhi are functions of the subtle body. When *tamas guna* is predominant we dream, when *rajas guna* is predominant we astral travel, and when *sattva guna* is predominant we are in samadhi. Dream sadhana is one of the methods to achieve astral travel, or even samadhi.

Can you get stuck in a place when doing astral travel?
Don't get inside a box!

We receive a dream by impressions. In our dreams we experience the five senses, but we have no control over them. There is a method of yoga by which one can control dreams.

If we do dream sadhana, does it take the place of regular sadhana?
Dream sadhana can be done in addition to regular sadhana. If you don't do regular sadhana you can't do dream sadhana.

What is the discipline?
Write down your dreams early in the morning every day for one year. This will develop awareness of dreams. After six months or a year, select the dreams that are linked or have been repeated several times, and try to dream those dreams one at a time. This will develop control over dreams. When you are able to dream what you want to dream, then try to dream of a place which you have visited. When that is successful, try to dream of a place you have not visited. This will

develop the power of astral traveling. After some practice, you can dream of doing yoga and meditation. Try to dream that your kundalini is awakening and all energy centers are opening up.

It takes concentration to dream what you want to dream. So before going to bed, concentrate on the subject that you want to dream. Meditate for four or five minutes on the thousand-petaled lotus, or on your luminous form; then bow to God and go to sleep.

Why do we forget our dreams?
To remember them is a sadhana—to keep them in mind and analyze them. If the dream is tamas guna predominant, we forget it.

How do we stop our thoughts at night so that we can sleep deeply?
First stop the thoughts in the day; then you can stop them at night.

Is life a dream or a meditation?
[Asked by a seven-year-old boy]
Life is a meditation when you know it is a dream.

Is symbolism in dreams only personal, or are there some universal symbols?
Some of each. Dreams of the elements are universal. For example, a dream of water means that the water element is predominating. It relates to the second chakra. Tamas guna controls the first and second chakras, rajas controls the third, and sattva controls the fourth and fifth chakras.

Is a dream acting out one's psyche?
Life is a dream. In a dream you dream your dream.

I once dreamt about some events that later came true. How could I have knowledge of the future?
In the superconscious state there is no past, present, or future. What you realized is that everything is inside. This is the realization that comes with samadhi. In pure dreams it can also be realized. Your dream was due to pure samskaras.

Do you sometimes see the future before you get to it?
Sometimes people get flashes of the future, and when the mind is purified one can see more.

Sometimes I see people and feel like I recognize them. Why?
Past is repeating in a samskara as the present. Because the past samskaras are presenting themselves in the present, so someone known in the past can appear as a known person in the present.

In a dream one year can be five minutes.

GURU

A guru is one who has wisdom
and is capable of
teaching.

The parents are the first gurus. The child goes to school, and the teachers there are the next gurus. Then one desires to attain peace and seeks a person who can show the way to find it. That is the spiritual guru. Above all these is the real guru, which is your own true Self. All gurus are merged in that guru. One who is established in the real Self doesn't need a physical guru.

Who can initiate?
Your faith. Initiation has no meaning if you have no faith. Once a guru teaching archery to the Pandava princes would not let a tribal boy become his student. The boy made a clay statue of the guru, practiced in front of it, and achieved greater success than the other students. It happened because his faith in that statue was so real. If you have faith in a guru, or in the image of a guru, it can give you the ability to finish the ego. Then you can experience God directly.

What reason is there to be around a guru if you have faith in God?
It is not important. When one realizes that knowledge can be attained by one's own sadhana, one's own Self becomes guru.

Is there no other way the guru can help?
The guru helps all the time. If you have full faith, then you are not two—you are one.

Do you have a guru in your tradition?
Yes, I have a guru.

Is your guru in his body?
For me, he is always in his body.

Can you communicate with him at will?
Yes, he is in me.

Will you explain what devotion to a teacher means?
Devotion to a teacher is to respect and to love that teacher. Attachment gets so dense that a person doesn't feel the difference between God and guru. And truly they are not different.

Are you talking about a teacher or a guru?
I am talking about God or guru. You can say, "This is a good driving teacher." You respect the teacher's driving ability and no more. I'm talking about quite a different thing—a teacher who is helping others to attain enlightenment.

What is the difference?
Working for food and working for enlightenment are not the same.

Should one have attachment for a teacher, for guru, for God?
Attachment to God is devotion, and devotion is important for enlightenment. Devotion is not a small thing; it affects many things.

Just as the ground is important for growing a seed, in the same way faith is the ground for yoga's growth. Faith is the real teacher, faith is the real yoga, and faith is the real attainment. We project our faith on some person as a teacher and we feel the teacher's love, peace, and wisdom inside us. If we don't project our faith on that person we won't feel anything. The teacher will be just another ordinary person.

A guru can only point toward a tree
and say, "Look, there is a bird sitting on a branch."
The guru's duty is finished and the student's duty begins.
The student tries to see the bird, moving the head up
and down and sideways, and now and then asks,
"Where is the bird?" The teacher again points
and says, "Look straight along my finger."
The student finally sees the bird.
The act of seeing is within,
but one needs to use one's vision
in the right manner.

I feel that the desire for and the attachment to a guru is very harmful and that one can't get beyond it.
That's true if you are trapped on a physical level. Poison kills and poison cures.

How can one recognize that a guru is enlightened, and is it important?
In one sense a guru is an ordinary person. You must have faith to feel the enlightenment. Faith brings grace. If you have faith in a garbage can, it can be your guru. Without faith you can see an enlightened person and get nothing. Realized and unrealized yogis are all the same in their bodies; the difference is in their consciousness. An enlightened yogi holds an apple on the hand, but the thought of apple is not in the mind; while an unenlightened yogi holds an apple on the hand and also in the mind. Both can do stupid things, but the actions of one who has a doer's ego create samskaras, whereas the other yogi remains free.

Can you, Babaji, recognize enlightened people?
Light never hides.

Can all recognize that light?
Not blind people.

You wrote that if a pickpocket sees a saint the pickpocket will only see pockets; what does a saint see?
A saint sees a saint.

Did you ever see anyone become enlightened through a gesture, a smile, or a touch?
I have seen enlightenment come by the ability of the person, not by the touch.

If an enlightened being can see what the future holds, then is it possible for that being to change or redirect the course of life by will?
An enlightened being has no separate will from God. There is no ego of being a doer. Anything that happens through that being is God's will.

Does an enlightened being repeat the life cycle?
If an enlightened being gets another body to be in the world, it is God's will, but the being acts like a shadow of God.

Some teachers say you don't have to do anything, just "be as you are."
It's a very simple thing to say, but if we really examine ourselves, then we often find we are not being our true Self. So we have to work hard to get to the state where there is no ego, attachment, or desires.

What do we surrender to God?
We surrender our ego. Surrender doesn't mean to become like a rock and not do anything.

The ship is steered by one rudder;
the rudder is within the ship. The guru is within you,
and that guru is your own Self.

In what sense do we surrender to guru?
When we project guru outside, we are really surrendering our ego-self to our real Self. But at first we need some reason to do that. A physical guru becomes such a reason.

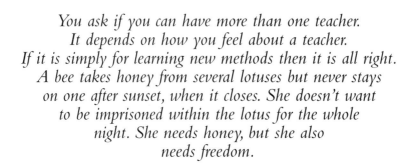

You ask if you can have more than one teacher.
It depends on how you feel about a teacher.
If it is simply for learning new methods then it is all right.
A bee takes honey from several lotuses but never stays
on one after sunset, when it closes. She doesn't want
to be imprisoned within the lotus for the whole
night. She needs honey, but she also
needs freedom.

Is it necessary to meet a guru to become a realized being?
If you find one it can help. Guru is your own real Self. Go inside and you will find.

Then why does guru manifest outside?
You are manifesting your world. God manifests God. It's all God, but we make it world. Your own desire is projecting it, and you are capable of finishing it. The natural form of a being is God, and the same being is the world when polluted by ego, desire, and attachment.

How important on a practical level is a guru?
Someone who understands your mental level can tell you which of the many yoga methods is right for you. Also, it is important to get support from someone whom you accept as higher. Another person can cook for you, but can't eat for you. Even a perfect master can't eat for you. It's good to have faith in a living master, but you must strive for it to achieve your aim. It's better to have faith in one's own Self. Without that, faith in a master won't remain long. Guru lies within, not without.

When a teacher is needed, is the teacher there?
Yes. Need made the airplane; it will make a teacher. But the need must be real.

Can we gain freedom without following a master?
All answers are inside us and we have to realize them by ourselves.

The whole world is a teacher and we are learning from everybody. It doesn't mean that one can understand everything at once. Some answers are very deep inside and some are not so deep. The higher the consciousness goes, the deeper the power of understanding goes. We are all different in our samskaras, our thoughts, and our senses. Because of these differences, we each take our own meaning out of the words of others and act accordingly.

Can we use the mind to know the mind, or do we need a perfect master?
We use a thorn to pry out a thorn; we use iron to cut iron. When we do yoga we use our minds to stop the thoughts. You can say it's using mind to stop the mind.

I feel we need a perfect master to take us the last step to God.
Attain highest consciousness by deep meditation, and this highest consciousness will be the perfect master.

When one realizes that knowledge can be attained through one's own sadhana, one's own Self becomes the guru. Everything becomes clear step by step.

For sadhana do asanas to keep the body fit, pranayama for purification of the nerve channels and the mind, and concentration for one-pointedness. If these three things are practiced regularly, then slowly one achieves higher consciousness. This higher consciousness is the guru. One who knows this secret remains in the state of cosmic consciousness forever.

LIBERATION

Just as pain will come, so will pleasure.
Just as hate will come, so will love. When both
are accepted, unaffected by the mind,
then there will be peace.

For how many years does one do a sadhana to get enlightenment?
It depends on the sincerity of one's aim. It can happen in a flash of light, but also it can take years, or even several births.

I've heard it said that a person can become too attached to practice.
We use medicine as long as we're not cured. After that we throw it away. Attachment to practice is important as long as the result is not obtained.

To search for enlightenment—is it like being ill? We search until we are cured?
We all are ill from illusion or ignorance. The world with desires is an illusion; without desires it is truth, love, God.

Is it really possible for anyone here to get enlightenment in this lifetime?
The state is already there; it only needs to be awakened.

What happens in your navel when you get enlightenment?
A lotus pops out! *[joking]*
Nothing happens in the physical body; it happens in the consciousness.

Is Zen enlightenment different from that of other paths?
Realization of truth is enlightenment. Truth can't be different for Buddhists, Hindus, Christians, or others. For me all sadhanas are the same if they are practiced for realization of God.

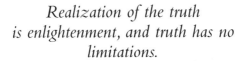

Realization of the truth
is enlightenment, and truth has no
limitations.

In God's creation everything is possible.
If one desires to be unattached one can be unattached,
and if one desires to be attached one can be
attached. The former will attain peace
and the latter will attain pain.
This is the only difference.

When you are awake, the dream is gone.
When you are enlightened,
maya is gone.

There are four doors to liberation:

1) *satsang*—association with the truth through meeting with spiritual people and reading spiritual books;

2) *vichara*—Self-inquiry, asking "Who am I?"

3) *santosha*—contentment in any situation, whether we gain or lose;

4) *samata,* equality—All are equal, from an insect to a saint, because *atman* in every being is the same and God lives in every being in the form of atman.

One door is enough to get in the house.
When you are in the house
all doors unite there.

Is it possible after enlightenment to wake and wonder what it's all about?
After enlightenment the past becomes unimportant.

Can we gain liberation through intellectual understanding of systems or theories?
There is no end to intellectual understanding. It doesn't give experience, just as memorizing the definition of liberation won't give liberation. The more we forget intellectual games, the more devotion we develop. In surrendering to God we don't have to read scriptures. We don't have to attend lectures of priests, saints, or psychologists. We just have to do it!

On the other hand, jñana yoga (yoga of knowledge) is one of the paths for attaining liberation. In this path the aspirant reads scriptures and studies the teachings of highly evolved beings. By this method the aspirant starts to understand the gross, subtle, and causal bodies, and the soul's relationship to these bodies. Then one attains the realization that the soul, or Self, is distinct and separate from all forms. This knowledge of the Self brings liberation.

What does it mean, "God is the Great Unmanifest"?

God is the creator of the world. We don't see the form. We don't know how God came into existence. Creation is God.

Is it possible to understand God without form?

It is easy to worship a form because we can see it and feel it. But God is beyond name and form. Our desire has created the form and we worship our desire. It's a good method, but after reaching a higher stage the name and form disappear. In worshipping God with form, you attain God according to your own vision. This illusion will take you to the true God. When I was a little boy I thought that God was like a giant who walked on the roof.

And now what do you think that God is like?

I don't think God has legs.

God is magic.
God lives in the heart.
We can't see God because our eyes
don't see inside ourselves.
But if you try to see inside yourself,
then you can see God.
God is not air, but air is a part of God.
God is not water, but water is a part of God.
God is not earth, but earth is a part of God.
Just like your nose is not you,
but it is a part of you.

. . . Letter to a child

God is the only lover and loves in different forms. Parent, husband, wife, friend, children, animals—all are God's forms and yet God has no form.

An aspirant attains the very God that is formed in the mind. If one thinks God is light, God appears as light. If one thinks God is sound, God appears as sound. If one thinks God has a human form, God appears in a human form. All of these appearances are illusions of the mind, but each illusion is true to the person who sees it, and it brings a conviction of truth. Actually, God is everything and nothing, beyond name and form.

When you start loving God,
you are not very far from God.

It is difficult for the average person to imagine a formless God.
Accept God in all forms and no form, and be happy. God is mother, yet we must take care of our own needs. God has arranged everything, and we must learn to accept everything. It is wrong thinking to expect God to come and put food in your mouth. But if you have surrendered the ego totally, then, like a small baby, your needs will be supplied.

How does one know that one is arriving at this surrender to God, and not just using the concept as an excuse to avoid responsibility?
First comes contentment, then dispassion. One doesn't feel anger, hate, jealousy; love is spreading everywhere. When these qualities appear, that is surrender to God.

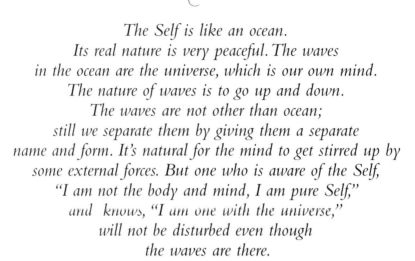

The Self is like an ocean.
Its real nature is very peaceful. The waves
in the ocean are the universe, which is our own mind.
The nature of waves is to go up and down.
The waves are not other than ocean;
still we separate them by giving them a separate
name and form. It's natural for the mind to get stirred up by
some external forces. But one who is aware of the Self,
"I am not the body and mind, I am pure Self,"
and knows, "I am one with the universe,"
will not be disturbed even though
the waves are there.

What is dispassion?
If you are happy not having anything, that is *vairagya,*
or dispassion. In samadhi a yogi gets vairagya, and if
after coming out of samadhi the yogi is still attached to
the world then it wasn't samadhi; it was no better than
sleep.

Dispassion doesn't mean to separate oneself
from people, but to understand that this world is not real.
Dispassion is attachment to God.

When a yogi gets dispassion, sometimes the thought
comes to leave the body. But to leave the body while
being in the body is real dispassion.

Dispassion is a state of mind in which one can live in
desires without desire.

Can one become dispassionate by desiring it?
Sometimes a person can get extreme dispassion
through samskaras or by the grace of God, and then
within seconds the chain of attachment breaks. It
happens to one person out of millions. Others can get
dispassion by regular practice of yoga. There is no set
amount of time for this attainment. It depends upon
truthfulness in yoga practices, faith, devotion, and the
strong will of an aspirant.

One who gets extreme desire for liberation becomes
worthy of liberation.

There are seven stages in yoga sadhana, according to the *Yoga Vasishtha*. As long as one is in the first three stages one can't be completely nonattached. The fourth stage gives complete knowledge of reality. As soon as one attains the fourth stage one no longer cares about the gross body, which functions simply by its samskaras and by reflex action. At that stage one is no longer the doer; so there will be no errors, no duties, no responsibilities. By the grace of God one can jump from the third to the fourth stage with regular practice.

1) *shubhechha* (virtuous desire): In the first stage, the yogi has extreme desire for enlightenment. By constantly discriminating between what is permanent and what is impermanent, the yogi strives to remove all pains caused by desiring worldly comforts.

2) *vicharana* (reflection): The yogi reflects deeply on the subtle meaning of the scriptures. One also studies and listens to teachings of the wise teachers, and reflects on one's own Self, by the Self-inquiry of "Who am I?"

3) *tanumanasa* (one-pointed mind): By regular practice of meditation, the mind becomes one-pointed and capable to understand the subtle aspect of an object.

These first three stages are called *jagrat bhumi,* or "stages of knowing the difference between *jiva*-hood and the Supreme Self (God)." But the yogi is still not enlightened. In these stages one achieves knowledge of the *tattvas* or elements, but remains in dualism.

4) *satvapatti* (experience of truth): The yogi experiences that God *(Brahman)* alone is truth, and that this creation is illusionary. It is the stage of a *siddha* or

perfected one. In this stage one still functions in the world, but knows that everything is an illusion except God, so the mind doesn't get trapped by the illusionary world.

5) *ashanshakti* (freedom from attachment): A yogi in this stage is completely free from all attachments and only identifies with God, or the Self. It is as if the aspirant has fallen asleep in the union of God, and wakes up only when asked to talk or answer questions about God.

6) *padarthabhavani* (non-perception of external world): In this stage the yogi remains merged in God for a longer period of time than in the fifth stage. This is the only difference.

7) *turyaga* (complete isolation, immersed in God): In this stage one doesn't wake up, either by one's own will or by others, but remains completely merged in the bliss of God. It is a complete non–dual state.

Stages four through seven bring knowledge of God, and that divine knowledge progresses more in each stage until the soul becomes completely one with God. That yogi is neither alive nor dead.

What is spiritual and what is material?
God and the world.

With what desire are we created? Why is the soul created?
The soul is not created by desires. It is like a shadow of God inside a being.

Self is God. But as long as we don't find God within ourselves there is a difference between God's will and our will. We need complete surrender to find God within ourselves. Complete surrender doesn't mean not to work, not to eat, not to meet people, but rather to eliminate the ego of "I am the doer" from the mind. What happens then? The mind begins to accept all situations and becomes free from pleasure and pain. It develops dispassion, and dispassion brings enlightenment. In words the method seems very easy, but to surrender is a very difficult thing. It needs constant practice. We have to watch our every action. Without watching ourselves we can't be aware of the tricks the mind plays. So a yogi should be alert all the time.

*A gold piece covered with dried mud
looks like a rock, but as soon as
the mud covering is broken
the gold piece shines and is clearly separate
from the mud. This body, the mind, the senses,
and their creation of worldly illusions
are like a covering on the Self.
They hide its glory,
but the Self is never really affected by them.
It is always separate, like a lotus leaf which,
when taken out of a pond,
doesn't retain
a single drop of water.*

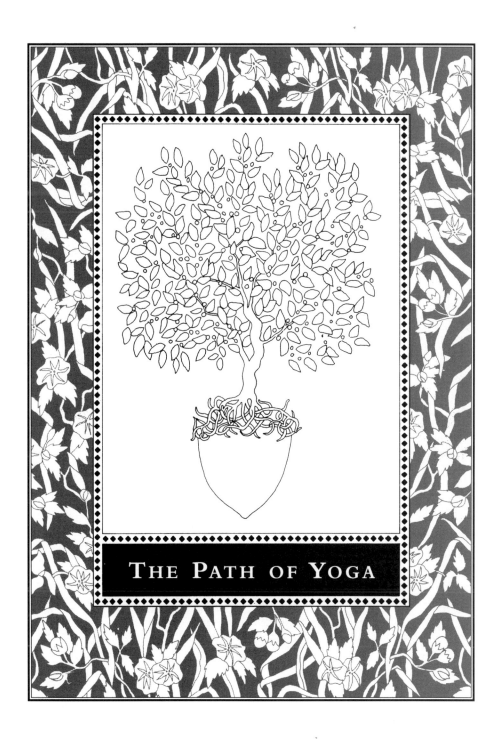

THE PATH OF YOGA

YOGA

That the world is untrue is satyam (truth).

To realize this truth is jñanam (knowledge).

Truth has no end, anantam (infinity).

Truth is the origin, Brahman (God).

All are the same.

Yoga is for attaining this truth.

A tree is inside a seed in subtle form. When the seed is sown the tree comes out in its physical form. In the same way all knowledge is already in our mind and by doing yoga this knowledge comes out.

We do yoga only on faith—from hearing others talk about it or by reading books. We really don't know what is happening or what will happen. It is like making a building in space. In yoga we strive from nothing to nothing. We create a belief in the existence of God, and this belief is mixed with doubts. So we make it stronger by faith, and we feed it with devotion. This whole process starts from the physical body, with the practices of *yama, niyama, asana,* and *pranayama.* Next we become conscious of the subtle body through the practices of *pratyahara, dharana, dhyana,* and *samadhi.** Then we merge into the causal body, which is called liberation.

To achieve benefits in yoga must one have faith?
Faith is one of the spiritual benefits that develops by doing yoga. Yoga also gives physical benefits. Aim is the most important thing. The greatest benefit is obtained from yoga if it is practiced for the sake of Self-realization.

Yoga is calming and pleasant if you build it up like a building. Do some each day; otherwise it will be a burden and you will run away. A musician works ten to twelve hours a day to learn music. Actually the method is learned in a day, but practiced hard for many years.

---

* These are the eight steps of ashtanga yoga. See page 100.

Are religions, particularly Christian religions, the same as yoga? Will reading the Bible, going to church, and so forth, bring the same results?
Yoga is not a religion. Religion and yoga are different things. You can do yoga and still practice your religion.

Which path do you advise people to follow— karma yoga or bhakti yoga?
Both are important for the spiritual path.

Just as one medicine can't cure all diseases, so one particular yoga can't help everyone. Each person is unique in nature, body structure, and *samskaras;* each has talents and each has handicaps. Some are born artists, poets, mathematicians, scientists, and a little practice opens the whole field of their knowledge. In the same way some are born liberated—understanding that they are pure Self, separate from all worldly illusions. They never identify with the body. Others are born without the slightest understanding of God, Self, peace. What they see and feel through their sense organs is reality to them. Yet through spiritual practice they can develop the understanding that there is something beyond body and mind.

There are four motivations for starting yoga:

1) pain *(arta)*,

2) desire for wealth and power *(artharthi)*,

3) desire to know God *(jijñasu)*,

4) one is born with dispassion *(jñani)*.

Of all these the first is the most common. Even Buddha turned toward Self-realization due to pain.

Yoga is a hard medicine. Its taste is bitter, but without taking it one can't get cured. For attaining peace, regular *sadhana* is the only medicine. Sometimes sadhana becomes as bitter as quinine, but the patient should take it anyway.

How can one do yoga when living with people who don't?

Some people can't do yoga even when living around those who do. If a person has dispassion *(vairagya),* yoga can be done anywhere. A leader can do yoga and also govern the country. Yoga trains the mind. We hear noise, people, quarrels, and so forth; but if we train the mind to ignore these things they don't bother us. It depends on our aim. Someone who wants to purchase things sees what is in the store, but a friend who goes along for company doesn't notice the things in the store.

Those who compete in the Olympics work hard, very hard; some win medals and some don't. Learning yoga is not difficult; but to work on yoga regularly is very difficult, because there is no immediate gain. This disheartens the yogi at times. But one who works regularly, even though not winning a gold medal, achieves a very high stage of consciousness. There is nothing to lose.

When you are in yoga all your actions become yoga, because you are aware of your actions. When you are aware of your actions you can't forget God. God is so vast and a being *(jiva),* who is so small, can meet God from any direction, but still can't reach the limit. So the methods of attaining an unlimited God are also unlimited. Those who say, "This is the only way to attain God," are in illusion.

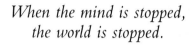

When the mind is stopped,
the world is stopped.

Yoga doesn't say not to do your social duties.
You should do all your duties toward society, but keep
your mind in yoga—like a circus performer
who walks the tightrope,
takes swings and performs several feats,
but always keeps her mind
on her balance.

Aim is the most important thing.

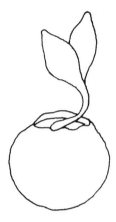

The mind *(chitta)* is like a vast field. This field is plowed
by good deeds and the soil is turned upside down. The
insects and weeds which live on the surface are like
the bad habits we have developed. They are buried
under the ground by the plow of good deeds. The
worms which live underground are like our samskaras,
tendencies from present and past births. They are
exposed above the soil and are eaten up by birds or are
consumed by the heat of the sun. When this field of
chitta is plowed again and again, the soil breaks up.
Then it must be irrigated by the practices of asana and
pranayama. The moisture from the irrigation rots the
buried weeds and insects, which makes the soil rich.
After that the seed of concentration (dharana) is sown
in that ground. Now we need to protect that seed, so
we fence it in with austerities, egolessness, and
peacefulness. This fence prevents encroachers and
animals (negative people or influences) from entering.
Contentment and tolerance work as guards which are
very alert to deter the enemies of expectation,
attachment, lust, greed, pride, and so forth. When the
seed of *sattva guna* sprouts, the weeds of *rajas* and *tamas*

gunas grow along with it. They try to cover up the tiny sprout, which is still very tender and small. Now again asana, pranayama, and meditation act as weeders; they cut back rajas and tamas gunas, and the sprout of sattva guna starts to grow. It grows two leaves—the goal and the path. Both leaves are fed from the same stem—sattva guna, or wisdom. Now this seed of concentration, which became a sprout, gets stronger and starts to branch. Truthfulness, contentment, egolessness, and compassion are the branches; and the plant becomes a tree which is strong enough to stand by itself. This tree is called samadhi. When the tree (samadhi) is mature, it starts to flower with dispassion. When dispassion reaches perfection it transforms itself into a fruit, which is knowledge of God. One who has attained this fruit is freed from the three-fold desire (fame, wealth, and sensual pleasure) and the three-fold karma (past, present, and future), and attains the stage of supreme dispassion, *kaivalya*.

ASHTANGA YOGA

*In sadhana
good and bad things happen.
Sometimes a yogi gets much faith and
sometimes loses faith.
If the aim is strong one doesn't quit
yoga sadhana, even when one loses faith.
Yoga sadhana is life. Once you start it,
go on doing yoga for your whole life;
and one day you will see that
all actions are yoga.*

The ancient sage Patanjali was the first to systematize the practices of yoga. He described yoga as a process having eight parts or "limbs"; thus the system is called ashtanga (ashta = eight, anga = limb) yoga. The eight limbs are: yama (restraints), niyama (observances), asana (postures), pranayama (control of *prana*, breath), pratyahara (withdrawing the mind), dharana (concentration), dhyana (meditation), and samadhi (superconsciousness).

YAMA-NIYAMA

Yama (restraint) consists of five parts: nonviolence *(ahimsa),* truthfulness *(satya),* non-stealing *(asteya),* sexual continence *(brahmacharya),* non-hoarding *(aparigraha).*

Niyama (observance) consists of five parts: cleanliness *(shaucha),* contentment *(santosha),* austerity *(tapas),* self-study *(svadhyaya),* surrender to God *(Ishvara-pranidhana).*

If one is observing yama and niyama (precepts of right living) in a perfect way, one doesn't need any other sadhana. But it's not so easy. As long as the consciousness is on a low level, yama and niyama are also on a low level. Yoga sadhana and yama/niyama reinforce each other. By observing yama and niyama one can develop the ability to do yoga, and by doing yoga one attains higher consciousness.

If you go deeply into any one of the five parts of yama, you will see that it covers the other four parts. It is the same with niyama. Suppose you take truthfulness, satya: By telling the truth, you are also practicing nonviolence (ahimsa), non-stealing (asteya), continence (brahmacharya), and non-hoarding (aparigraha).

One can't be completely truthful unless one observes the other four parts of yama. Then finally everything, yama and niyama, dissolves into total surrender to God, Ishvara pranidhana—the final niyama.

What does Babaji feel about tapas (austerity)?
To observe yama and niyama (reducing desires) is the only true tapas. The purpose of tapas is to detach the mind from the body. To hang upside down, sit on thorns, sleep on dirt, live naked, and so forth, is tapas only on a gross physical level. Tapas is not penance; it's a mental training to develop will power. There are thousands of kinds of tapas. According to the mental level of an aspirant, one is given a particular kind of tapas to help train the mind. To watch yourself is the hardest tapas.

ASANA

Is doing asanas the same as doing physical exercises—pushups, running, etc.?
Asana is not merely physical exercise. It's a union of mind (concentration), body movement, and breath. In physical exercise we work like a machine to develop muscles and muscular strength. In asanas the mind concentrates on the movement or on certain points of the body. Each movement has a pattern of inhalation and exhalation. The slower the movement, the more mind, body, and breath will be in tune. In this way asana makes a perfect union (yoga); it is a meditation. Asanas do not build a huge muscular body, but they give enormous physical benefits and mental strength. Asanas rejuvenate and tone the glands which control growth and all bodily and mental functions. So by doing asanas one can overcome physical weakness and maintain good health.

*Austerity means effort
to control desire. It is chosen, not forced.
Doing your duty is also tapas
when you watch your attachments
and self-interest and try
to remove them.*

PRANAYAMA

What is pranayama and its purpose?
Pranayama is breath control. It is not simply inhalation and exhalation. There is awareness of inhalation and exhalation, which means breath and mind are working together. Otherwise it would be easy to hike one mile each day and get the benefit of pranayama. The purpose of pranayama is to make the breath shallow. When the breath is shallow, the mind becomes still.

I worry about suffocating when the breath stops.
When breath becomes shallow through pranayama, it also becomes very smooth; there is no pressure at all. There is no suffocation in samadhi; this is a misconception. If a person increases pranayama little by little it is very effective, but if one does a lot one day and then stops for ten days it is very harmful. It can weaken digestion and upset the entire system.

Yoga sadhana is for stopping unnecessary thoughts. There are two methods to control thoughts: either control thoughts by your will power, or control them by doing pranayama regularly, which creates a situation where thought stops by itself. Don't try to fight with your thoughts; they will become more furious. First make yourself strong by doing regular sadhana.

In pranayama we practice deep inhalation, holding the breath, and complete exhalation. By this deep breathing we can hold the breath for a longer and longer time, saving pranic energy and exhaling less. With regular practice of pranayama a time is reached when we inhale, hold, and do not exhale. This stage is called samadhi. Pranayama is one of the methods of reaching samadhi. There are thousands of methods.

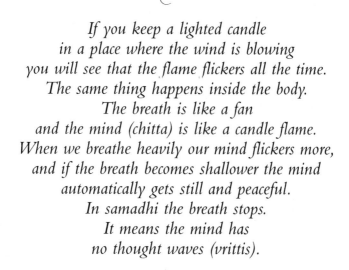

If you keep a lighted candle
in a place where the wind is blowing
you will see that the flame flickers all the time.
The same thing happens inside the body.
The breath is like a fan
and the mind (chitta) is like a candle flame.
When we breathe heavily our mind flickers more,
and if the breath becomes shallower the mind
automatically gets still and peaceful.
In samadhi the breath stops.
It means the mind has
no thought waves (vrittis).

Pratyahara

What is pratyahara?
Withdrawing the mind from objects which attract the senses is pratyahara. When the senses are withdrawn into the mind, then the next three stages of yoga can begin—concentration (dharana), meditation (dhyana), and superconsciousness (samadhi).

In the beginning when we practice pratyahara we have to avoid objects of pleasure in order to save ourselves from creating a desire to have them. This is called austerity (tapas). But when we master pratyahara, then we can live in desires without desire. We observe all social rules, but our mind is not attached to anything. Our balance becomes so perfect that we can function in the world without a thought of balancing.

You learn to ride a bicycle. In the beginning you fix your eyes on the road, keep the handlebars straight and firm, turn the pedals smoothly, and try to keep your balance. You have to think of many things at one time. But once you learn, you do it all without thinking about balancing, pedaling, steering—everything becomes automatic.

Dharana, Dhyana, Samadhi

When the mind is drawn in from the outer world (pratyahara) for twelve seconds the state is called dharana. When dharana continues for twelve times twelve seconds (two minutes, twenty-four seconds) dhyana begins. When dhyana continues for twelve times twelve times twelve seconds (twenty-eight minutes, forty-eight seconds) it is called lower samadhi (*samprajñata samadhi*).

When concentration (dharana), meditation (dhyana), and superconsciousness (samadhi) are all practiced together, it is called *samyama*. To get to the stage of samyama depends entirely on the practice of an aspirant. It becomes so automatic that as soon as the aspirant sits in meditation, consciousness begins to shift from dharana to dhyana to samadhi very swiftly.

To do regular yoga sadhana is difficult. Very few people do it. When asana, pranayama, and *mudra* are practiced regularly then one gains the ability to do concentration, meditation, and samadhi all together, which is called samyama. As soon as a yogi has the ability to do samyama, the yogi's practice becomes perfected. Another way is the Zen method, which is called dhyana yoga, or ch'an in Chinese. Through this system the mind is trained to do samyama directly. In earlier times the head of a Zen monastery would admit only students who were able to start at this stage. Ashtanga yoga, however, is for everybody.

CONCENTRATION (DHARANA)

When I concentrate on *ajña chakra* I seem to see a blue spot hovering in space outside my head. The dot of blue color you see in *ajña chakra* is the center, or *bindu*. Sometimes concentration on this makes it disappear, but regular practice of concentration will make it appear and stay. Then go deep inside it; you will see light, very bright light. Although we say the location of ajña chakra is behind the eyebrows, it is very subtle. It exists in a form of light and energy, which can be felt. The blue spot you were seeing outside your head was also right; in concentration the blue spot sometimes appears outside, which is the projection of the blue spot inside.

Concentrate very deeply on the blue spot, inside or outside, and it will give you peace and bliss.

Can you suggest specific methods for improving concentration in meditation?

Watching the breath is a very good method for developing concentration. It can be practiced all of the time. After a while one can develop awareness of breath even in sleep. If you watch it carefully you will notice that first you inhale and when you have taken a full breath there is a short pause; then you exhale, and after exhalation the breath again stops for a short time. If you make a deliberate effort to stop the breath at the top of the inhale, the method is more effective. The breath should be slow, gentle, regular, and without sound.

Is it good to do *mantra* and concentrate on ajña at the same time?

That is the method of mantra yoga—the union of mind, breath, and sound at ajña.

What is the difference between mantra and *japa?*

Mantras are sounds or words which have power due to the vibration of the sounds themselves. *Japa* is the rhythmic repetition of a mantra or name of God. It creates automatic pranayama, concentration, and meditation. The main idea in doing japa is to make the mind thoughtless. Then body consciousness disappears automatically. The body is the medium of sadhana and the body is the hindrance in sadhana. If your body consciousness disappears, it means your sadhana is going well.

Japa is a formal method of worshipping God. It should be done privately and preferably with a *mala,* or rosary.

Ajapa, "without repetition," is a method in which mind, mantra, and breath are so well attuned that the mantra repeats inside by itself—continuously and without conscious effort. This method can be practiced anywhere at any time, even in sleep.

In ajapa pranayama there is no retention of breath. Inhalation and exhalation are natural, with the mind fixed on *ham-sah.* Ham is the energy of Shiva, and sah is the energy of Shakti, so the two sounds encompass God and all of creation. By doing ham-sah continually the breath becomes shallow.

For practicing ajapa one takes a deep breath and then exhales, making the exhalation twice as long as the inhalation. After doing this for a few times one can breathe in a natural way, inhaling on ham and exhaling on sah. In exhalation the sound of sah can be prolonged.

When ham-sah ham-sah ham-sah is repeated often enough it becomes sah-ham, with sah on the inhale and ham on the exhale. In Sanskrit there are rules of elision called *sandhi*. When the sound of *visarga* (aspirate, in this case the "h" at the end of sah) comes before a consonant it changes into an "o" sound. So sah-ham becomes so-ham.

When so-ham so-ham so-ham so-ham is repeated enough, the "s" and "h" drop and all that remains is *Aum* or *Om*.

This mantra works on the different levels of all the bodies: ham sah is the gross level; so ham, the subtle level; Om, the causal level. It all happens by itself when an aspirant regularly practices ajapa.

Would living in a cave help my concentration, help me to get away from all the noise and confusion in my house?
If a person is living in a cave with the mind attached to the outer world, then the person is not in a cave. It's good to do sadhana in a cave for some time, but your cave is inside of you. Why don't you concentrate on *anahata,* the heart chakra? It is the emotional center and will take you to the same place as ajña. Concentrating on the heart center increases the emotions; if you feel it works better for you, it is not necessary to concentrate on other places.

MEDITATION (DHYANA)

What is meditation and is it necessary for enlightenment?
Meditation is for stopping thoughts. It is an important method to remove the pain of our own illusion.

There is no peace in the world.
If there is any peace it is only in meditation.
At first everyone does false meditation;
while you sit different kinds of thoughts come.
But this false meditation turns into true meditation
by regular practice.
One should not be afraid of the thoughts,
but try to eliminate them slowly.

Although there are millions of methods of yoga, the aim of all of them is to make the mind free from thought waves. For this, meditation is the most important thing. But it's not easy to meditate because of obstacles that come in the way. There are two main obstacles. First, the physical body—weakness, illness, stiffness, and so on. Second, samskaras—impressions of past and present actions which create tendencies toward present and future actions. The physical hindrances can be helped by doing asanas every day and by eating pure *(sattvic)* food. But the obstacles due to samskaras are very strong. One is drawn to the wrong path, and even though that is clearly understood, one can't stop oneself. Gambling, drug addiction, thoughts of hurting others, and all desires are impurities of the mind. The mind is purified in two ways—by doing pranayama and meditation, and by cultivating positive qualities. For developing positive qualities, an aspirant practices selfless action, associates with spiritual people *(satsang),* studies scriptures, and reads life histories of saints.

When the body works, the mind gets rest; and when the body rests, the mind becomes more active. This is the reason why when you want to meditate your mind creates more thoughts—strange thoughts, unbelievable thoughts—and you may become discouraged and want to stop meditation. This stage remains for six to twelve months. After that, if you are sincerely trying to meditate, your mind will disregard those thoughts.

When I meditate my mind is quiet at first. After a while I begin to daydream. How can I get through this?
It's the pull of the world. For a long time this happens, and then gradually the mind gets detached from the world and daydreaming stops. In meditation you can go deeper and deeper but as soon as you think, "This is it!" you're standing on the earth again.

A cotton thread can cut an iron bar
if passed over it daily.
If you work on yoga, yoga will work on you.

The different methods of meditation are just for tricking the mind out of its normal activity into a state of quiet. The meditator is ajña, the chakra in the forehead. In any technique you use, the meditator will not change; so if the meditation is done on ajña it is more direct. If you meditate on a rock or on something else, it is still ajña meditating. If the rock is not in ajña, you cannot see it. Anything you see or feel is the function of ajña. It is the seat of *manas,* one of the four aspects of mind.

*One who is pretending to sleep
can't be awakened. You know your mental games.
You know how you make yourself sad and miserable.
There is no medicine or mantra for that
except to kick yourself
and stop pretending to sleep.
To meditate for the purpose of getting high
is not meditation; it's simply an emotion.
If you meditate for peace,
which is calming the thought waves
of the mind, then you can attain
some reality.*

Why do you say one should meditate alone?

During concentration, when the mind is free from thoughts *(vrittis)*, it draws in worldly vrittis, just as a vacuum bottle sucks air when the cork gets loose. If concentration is very deep, then the mind doesn't draw in vrittis from the outside; but as soon as the concentration weakens, the mind fills with worldly vrittis. Then the aspirant is unable to draw in the mind again, at least for some time.

Is meditation helpful to everyone?

If you really meditate. If the mind goes to the bakery to purchase bread while you meditate, it won't help. Try to stop the mind for five minutes; then you will feel bliss. Meditation is a result of sadhana. If your practice goes well then meditation will come by itself—the mind starts going inward without any effort. No one can teach meditation; it is an action inside your mind and only you can know what you are doing. If I say concentrate on ajña you may not understand what I mean by my words, and I can't see what you are doing. But if what I say has some meaning for you and you do it, you will get it. If a person reads one hundred books on yoga, can the person concentrate better? The main thing is to practice.

I've had initiation into *shabda*. Can you discuss its relationship to ashtanga yoga?

Shabda means sound. When the body and mind are purified by regular pranayama and *shat karma,** or by meditation, then a kind of sound which already exists

---

* Shat karma consists of six practices for cleansing the inner as well as the outer body.

inside the body becomes louder and can be heard inside the ear. It is called *nada* or shabda. The sound changes into light in its advanced stage. It can be heard by deep concentration on ajña chakra or anahata chakra.

Actually this sound is a vibration of the *nadis* (subtle nerve channels) which we can feel inside our head and heart, but our external hearing process is by the ears so we identify it as in the ears. The sound should appear in the right ear and you should concentrate there. If it appears in the left ear you should try to switch it to the right ear. After some months' practice the sound switches to the top of the head, and then you have to concentrate on that spot.

The inner sound, or "unstruck" sound *(madhyama nada),* comes from the heart chakra. There are various different sounds: bee, flute, conch, sitar or other stringed instrument, bell, drum, bugle, ocean, waterfall, rumbling of clouds. When inner sound appears it shows that the nadis are becoming purified. If the mind concentrates on one sound, the sound will change to another, more subtle sound.

If one sound continues for several days, try to deliberately change it. For changing the sound you have to use will power. By deep concentration on one nada you can hear its subtler form which is like its echo. Sometimes you can become attached to hearing a certain sound; then you have to make the effort to change it to one of the other sounds. The next more subtle stage *(pashyanti nada)* comes from *svadhishthana chakra.* In this stage, the sound turns into light. The highest stage *(para nada)* comes from *muladhara chakra,* and appears as a loud clap of thunder, or Om in its pure state.

Nada is a purified state of mind. The more pure the mind, the clearer and more subtle the nada will become. In this way the mind dissolves into nada and samadhi is attained.

SAMADHI

What is samadhi?
Samadhi is an extremely dispassionate state of mind. The mind doesn't have any thoughts or ideas of present, past, or future. In that stage the mind totally disappears and is replaced by superconsciousness, God. Even in meditation you can begin to feel it. After the first samadhi the world is different. You see the illusory nature of objects. You still see an object, but you see it differently. Samadhi brings dispassion.

Thoughts, senses, and mind reinforce each other and keep us attached to the world. But when one is stopped, the other two stop by themselves. For this we do yoga. As soon as attachment to thoughts is given up, samadhi is attained.

Desires keep us in the body. Extreme desirelessness is samadhi. When samadhi becomes more dense the physical body also disappears.

Can you say something about losing body consciousness?
In deep concentration a person loses awareness of the outer surroundings and also of the body, just as a chess player is unaware of outside things while playing.

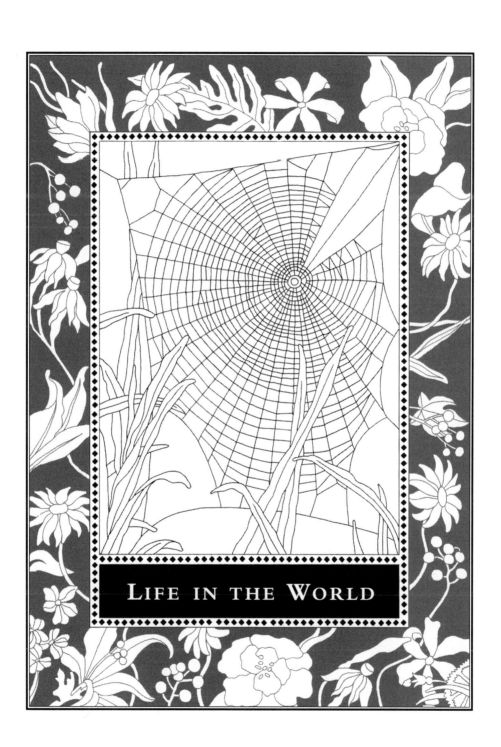

LIFE IN THE WORLD

Ego

Ego cannot be stopped,
only reversed. It can flow toward the world
or it can flow toward God.

How do you define ego?
Ego is life. To keep the body's existence is ego. It is the part of the mind which identifies us with the world. Ego-self tells you, "This is my body," and also tells you, "This is my Self." It connects the two. Without ego you couldn't understand the Self. Ego is the vehicle which can take you to the bliss sheath and by which you can reach enlightenment.

There are three kinds of Self:

Supreme Self—God, the purest form;
Self—the reflection of God inside the being;
Ego-self—identifies the being *(jiva)* with the world.

God is another name for truth.
In search of truth a person must understand
that existence in the world
is ego.

Ego manifests itself on three levels:

On the gross level there is *tamasic* ego—negativity, lust, anger, hate, jealousy, and so on; the mind is overpowered by its passions.

On the subtle level there is *rajasic* ego—a mixture of negative and positive qualities; the mind is filled with desires for power, and also compassion.

On the causal level there is *sattvic* ego—all positive qualities; the mind is filled with dispassion and desire to attain the truth.

Ego can move in two directions. When the ego is channeled toward the Self, it becomes sattvic ego, which is always good; when it is channeled toward the world, it is called tamasic ego, which makes illusion.

Ego is the bridge between the subtle body and the Self. The Self can be felt by some part of the ego, otherwise we wouldn't have any desire for God or liberation.

It seems the game gets subtler.
The ego also gets higher as your stage of consciousness gets higher. The ego can even trap you by being kind, generous, honest. We must be aware of that at all times.

To transcend the ego seems hopeless.
Watching the ego becomes a habit; you have to become as alert as a thief. You can stop an action if you really think it's not good.

That's another judgment—"good."
You don't grab a burning coal. We are trapped again and again because we can't really discriminate between good and bad. We always discriminate according to our desires.

Is it possible to use ego as a channel?
Without the ego you can't step forward. Ego is action. Without action you can't do anything. When you say, "I have to meditate," this is all action—ego.

So the idea is to purify ego?
Ego gets thinner and thinner, as a black cloud becomes a white cloud, and then the white cloud thins to a fine mist, and through that mist you can see. It doesn't obstruct your vision as much.

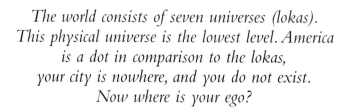

*The world consists of seven universes (lokas).
This physical universe is the lowest level. America
is a dot in comparison to the lokas,
your city is nowhere, and you do not exist.
Now where is your ego?*

What about ego getting in the way of *sadhana*?
What ego?

Oh, like saying, "Far out!" when I have a good meditation.
It's okay. Don't worry about ego; just meditate.

Is ego innate or learned?
Ego is life. Ego is the teacher. It is the way nature is set up. Everything is controlled by the ego. If a person is totally egoless, the five elements of the body split apart and there is no more body. Ego is the root of everything. The whole universe is created by ego.

The body, including the mind, is made up of the five elements—earth, water, fire, air, and ether. The Self is the witness of all these and is consciousness, itself. When ego dissolves in the Self, the body and this world (illusion) both disappear. That is called liberation.

So in real observation of the universe there is no separation between inside and outside?
The body makes the separation; when the ignorance of body disappears, there is no separation.

Then there is the possibility of enlightenment every minute, but we get distracted?
Yes. Our feelings for the gross [physical] level seem more real to us and this creates distraction.

The seer and the object seen form an illusory relationship. If the seer loses the ego of being a seer, then the object seen is free of illusion. There remains a reality—unchangeable, indestructible, immortal—which is God.

Once Ramakrishna Paramahansa said,
"A doll made of salt tried to fathom the ocean,
but dissolved on the way."

There is no end.
The farther we go, the farther
we have to go. It is the ego that says,
"Look what hard austerities I am doing,
what hard sadhana I am doing,
how much love and compassion I have."
In comparison to the endlessness of God,
everything in a human being is not
even one grain of sand
on a vast beach.

Everything we see in this world is personal. We are connected to each other by projection: I am in your illusion; you are in my illusion. Individually the illusion is personal—I project mine and you project yours. Ego in its tamasic state equals illusion, or manifestation of the world. We try to give understanding to the illusion by giving names. You gave rock a name. Rock never said, "I am a rock."

You advocate will power—through the will I will overcome this, etc. Isn't this more ego?
As long as we are the doer, everything is ego. Ego is the only thing that keeps us alive in the world. Development of positive ego power is will power.

What is free will?
You are free to grab a hot iron or jump from a cliff. You know it is dangerous. If you do it and say it is the will of God, that is wrong. God has given you a mind, and the mind is also guided by some super power. So we have free will and we don't have free will, like a goat tied with a long rope. It can roam a good distance, but at some point it comes to the end of the line.

What is the difference between ego effort and divine will?
By ego effort we reach the true Self. When ego-self dissolves into the true Self, everything becomes God's will.

It's hard to believe in God's will when the world is full of war and famine.
Belief in God's will is not for weak people.

The ego of free will keeps the world going on and on. Without it, all actions would stop. All our actions in the world, in the waking or in the dream state, are controlled by the ego-self. This ego-self is like a bridge which joins the individual soul (jiva) with the Self. Ego-self identifies the jiva with the true Self and also identifies jiva with the world. The Self is beyond pleasure and pain. All frustration, anxiety, pain, and pleasure is in the ego-self's control. All impressions of our actions in the present and past births *(samskaras)* are hidden in this ego-self, and they cause the continuing cycle of birth and death. The ego-self also controls the intuitive flashes one gets in the waking and dream states. The more ego-self goes toward the Self, the more intuitive knowledge becomes clear; the more ego-self goes toward the world, the more intuitive knowledge gets hazy.

Ego is important for achieving success in the world, but if directed this way it can be a great obstacle to attaining real peace. We are social beings; we can't live without the world. And to function in the world we need existence, or ego. Under such conditions how can we get peace? We can get peace if we learn to live among people unattached. If we understand that the world is unreal and only a projection of our ego, and if we act in the world only as if performing our duty, then there will be peace everywhere.

The three worst traps for the ego are: desire for sensual objects, desire for wealth, and desire for fame. Of these three, fame is the hardest to overcome and the last attachment to go.

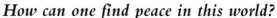

How can one find peace in this world?

*As long as we have the ego of being a doer, we can't be free.
Diving for pearls is easy, but when you have pearls you
develop fear of losing them. There is no peace.
So diving for God is better, although harder.
Peace, or freedom, can be attained by surrendering to God.
Do your sadhana (spiritual practice) regularly and offer it
to God. Don't do it to attain powers or knowledge.
Do it as a humble servant of God, without
expecting reward. Do it as a woman who gathers flowers
from the garden to make a garland for her beloved,
and puts it around his neck when he comes.
Her beloved's happiness is her happiness.*

DESIRES

Desire makes more desire
and in this way the whole world is formed.
This spider web of desire is inside
us and spreads outside.
Just like a spider, we weave the
web and we can also
swallow it.

Attachment to the world (my house, my garden, my son) and the ego of "I am the doer" (doctor, lawyer, minister, yogi) chain up human beings so tightly that we don't want to lose the attachment, even though we know that when it is gone we will attain eternal peace. We choose to remain in the pain of "I am the doer."

Where does desire originate?
The desires we have are actually samskaras. They are formed in this way:

1) You associate with an object, and feel you possess it.

2) You are no longer in association with the object, and even though it is not present, it stays as an image in the mind.

3) Your mind creates a craving for the object.

4) The craving makes a print in the mind (samskara) which remains even after death.

Desire is the third stage. We're not aware of the first two stages; they are too subtle. In the next birth, samskaras recreate desires automatically. You could get the desire to steal even though you were brought up in a good family. You won't necessarily understand where that desire came from. The desire develops more when it is fulfilled.

Desires can be overcome by controlling them; we have to put a limit on desires. By limiting desires they will change. You will start to desire to attain God rather than the world.

Why should we avoid desires if we don't hurt anyone else or ourselves?
Desire makes desire. It has no limit. When desires are limited it gives peace.

Aren't we born to experience these desires?
Desire and the world are the same thing. Attachment is a rope which binds desires and the world (sensual objects) together. We create this world by our desires and we are capable of getting out of it. But it is not easy to do unless we develop extreme dispassion. For developing dispassion, we have to play all those tricks called yoga.

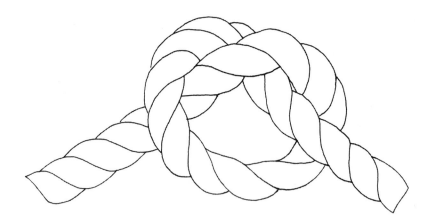

Can we free ourselves from desires through acting them out but watching them happen?
There is desire with attachment and desire without attachment, which is called dispassion. No one can be totally desireless; we are alive because we desire to live. Be in your desire without desire.

How can one know which desires to act on and which just to watch?
Some desires, like hunger, are important to keep the body alive to do one's duties. Some desires are not important but they possess our minds very much in order to please the senses. We should watch those desires.

Somehow, living on this planet with this body, I feel these senses should be pleased.
Senses can be pleased by drugs, and drugs can kill the senses. But if we use our senses in the right way we can be happy in the world.

What about other things, like sex?
What is the limit? You have to keep a limit in order to enjoy sex, otherwise it will also kill you.

But if you have a desire for something . . .
Switch the mind, or learn by burning the fingers that fire is hot.

All successful people have had the desire to achieve. Without this desire they would not have done anything. What about this?
That desire was important because first they made an aim and then dissolved themselves to follow that aim. You can't work without desire.

A saint lived in a jungle. One day another saint came and gave him a book, the *Bhagavad Gita*. The saint would read the book daily. One day he saw the book had been chewed on by rats. He decided to keep a cat to control the rats. He kept a cat, but the cat needed milk to drink. So he kept a cow. Then he could not look after all these animals by himself, so he married a woman to help him. After two years in that jungle he had a big house, a wife, two babies, cats, cows, and so on. Now the saint became worried. He thought about how happy he had been when he was alone. Now instead of thinking about God, he was thinking about his wife, children, cow, and cats. He began to ponder on how it all happened, and he came to the conclusion that one tiny book had made such a big world.

How do we get rid of our desires?

For maintaining the body, a few needs are natural and some desires are not important. You can reduce your desires gradually.

Desire is life. If there are no desires at all, then we can't function in the world. Poison in a proper dose cures a disease, but if taken in an overdose it kills. Desire kills when you are trapped in desire.

Desirelessness doesn't mean
to become like a rock—without love,
without emotions, without doing your duties in life.
It's only a stage in which inwardly we don't
feel "I am this," or "I am that,"
and outwardly everything
goes on as usual.

People say one should rid oneself of desire. But what if desire is for God?

That desire is devotion. Desire to seek truth is a sattvic desire. Spiritual desire is part of truth.

Desire creates all of the objects that are in your life. The only escape from the trap is to realize that the objects and conditions of your life are illusions projected by you. So why identify with them?

Why are we so attached to the physical plane if it is illusion?

Because nature needs attachments to evolve.

*Yoga is a method by which a person develops
higher consciousness. It gives an ability to understand the
reality of the world. When this reality is realized, then
a person is released from a self-created prison.
Ninety-nine percent of us are in prisons.
We imprison ourselves by building walls of desires,
attachments, needs, and demands. Then we
live in pain for our whole life.*

*The past is dead. Forget it. The future is uncertain,
so don't dwell on it. The present can be blissful if you
accept everything that comes as God's will.*

. . . From a letter to a man in prison

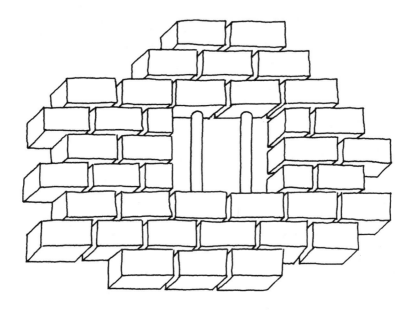

Why are we separated from God?

When a human being takes birth and the mind starts to develop, sensual pleasures of the world are experienced. In the next birth the sensual desires increase, and in the next they increase more. It's like a flow of water which runs downward. It encourages reproduction and the continuation of the world. At the same time it puts a curtain between the individual soul (jiva) and God.

Is it because God wants it to happen? Is God the one making the trouble?

God is not making the trouble; we are making the trouble. God gives us food but we overeat.

Why does a person become discontent?

Discontentment is created when desires are not fulfilled. It takes various forms, but the three primary expressions of discontentment are eating, clinging (possessiveness), and attachment. As soon as one takes birth one wants to eat, so eating is the first natural tendency in a being. When one develops a sense of discontentment one begins to eat without considering needs (gluttony). The second natural tendency in a being is to own the objects the senses are attracted to. When one develops a sense of discontentment one clings to more and more things (possessiveness). It gives a feeling of closeness with an object and a sense of ownership. When the senses are attracted to an object the mind develops desire for it (attachment). This attachment causes loss of discriminative power, which creates delusion. This delusion wipes out all memory of a higher Self and makes ignorance, which causes gluttony, lust, deceit, anger, covetousness, jealousy, hate, and pride.

The search for liberation begins by developing contentment which controls these eight demons. When all these demons are controlled, then automatically desires are controlled. When desires are controlled, the ego of existence is eliminated and a being becomes immortal.

Be in the world, but not of the world.
Be alone among people.

One can only be free from the demons of fear, anger, and pain by living in this world unattached, desireless. It's difficult, but living in the world with desires is not easy either. If both are difficult, then we may as well try to unwind ourselves from the trap, rather than to wind it more tightly. The traps of the external world are grosser traps and can be avoided by various methods, but the traps of the world inside the mind are very subtle, and are much more difficult to overcome.

We live in the imagination of others. When we see a person, we don't see the reality of that person—we see only our projected desires, which is our imagination. In this way, as long as we have not yet realized the truth, we all live in the imagination of each other.

By becoming aware of how desires control our actions, samskaras become thinner and thinner until they are transparent.

Desire creates more desire.
The whole world goes on in this way.
The silkworm makes a net to imprison itself. In
the same way we make a net of attachments, desires,
possessiveness around ourselves and we sit
inside that net in pain and depression.
As long as the net is intact the silkworm remains
dormant, but as soon as it is broken the silkworm comes
out in the new form of a butterfly, which can fly and
make everyone happy. In the same way, if we
break our self-created net of desires and
attachments we will become one
with our true nature.

What is pleasure and what is pain?

A kind of experience accepted by the mind is called pleasure, and when that experience is rejected by the mind it changes to pain. Pleasure and pain are self-created illusions. The world itself is an illusion, and we have to go through all these pleasures and pains to attain the truth. When pleasure continues for a time it gives a feeling of happiness. But there is no real pleasure in this world. Material possessions can't protect us from pain. Desires, attachments, and pain keep the machine of the world running. If these stopped, everything would stop and the world would be dead.

Why is there pain in this world?

If you think about this deeply you will come to the conclusion that it exists because we search for pleasure. The mind compares, "This is pleasure, and that is pain." Pleasure and pain are nothing but the mind's acceptance and rejection of experience.

Does pain come from trying to hang onto things?

Non-acceptance of life is pain. For instance, when one gets older and does not accept age, there is pain.

Yes. But is there not an easy way to get out of pain?

By acceptance. It's only a matter of switching the mind.

How does one understand on more than an intellectual level?

Intellectual understanding is like seeing New York on a map. You have to be there to experience it. For that one needs sadhana.

Understanding can only be clear
when there is dispassion (nonattachment).
If there is attachment, we will
understand desire instead of truth.
That is delusion.

Must you let go of compassion in order to have dispassion?
There are three stages: passion—desire for sensual objects; compassion—desire for helping others; and dispassion—beyond both. There are three ways of playing life's game: first, with passion, which starts as soon as the sense of "me" and "mine" develops, very young in life. Next, we develop compassion by using the discriminative mind. And finally, dispassion develops on the foundation of compassion.

What is the relationship of passion to love?
Passion is completely related to the senses, and love is related to the pureness of heart.

And compassion?
Compassion is the desire to help others. It is still related to the senses. But dispassion is beyond both passion and compassion. When faith, devotion, and right thinking are developed it is called *vairagya,* a stage of dispassion. A person gets dispassion from the world because higher consciousness brings the understanding that the world is an illusion, or *maya.* One who doesn't identify with sensual objects is unattached, desireless, and content.

Desirelessness is bliss.

Live in desires without desire.
There is no technique, only understanding.

One who doesn't desire anything
owns everything.

Anger and violence never work to win the heart of any creature. Even in taming an animal we use love. Attachment is not bad if it is used to live peacefully together. When we are in a society, or in a family, we need attachment, ego, desires—but within limits. Detachment should be realized in the mind, and not simply by throwing away things, being silent or anti-social.

How can we see our attachments that interfere with developing dispassion?

You can feel attachment in all your actions. If a child hides your shoe, you will get upset. You will not say, "I am upset because I am attached to my shoe," but you are. As soon as you are aware of your attachments they become like a TV show. You can see the whole drama in your head.

How can I get rid of attachment?

We are attached because we want to be attached. As long as we want to get pleasure from the world, attachment is needed. Without attachment we can't enjoy the world.

What can I replace my attachments with?

Attachment to God.

How?

You have to experience God to get attached.

FEELINGS
& EMOTIONS

*You should think that all
actions are for God. So your garden is for God,
you eat for God, and your life is for God. When this
thought becomes deeper you will find that
God is everywhere
and all your actions are meditation.
Gradually the chains of anger, hate, jealousy will
loosen, and one day you will be free
and fly away.*

You ask, "What is fear?
What is anger? What is pain?"
The root of fear, anger, and pain is ignorance.
Ignorance is accepting the world as real.
If you dream that a snake is chasing you, you run
and cry due to fear. The dream is real as long as you
are asleep. But when you wake up you don't cry
because you know the dream was not real.
The world is only as real as a dream;
when awakened it is
no longer real.

I understand emotion is important on the *bhakti* path, but can you have emotion with dispassion?
Dispassion is not a lack of emotion, but a lack of attachment. What is love? Do you think that a person who has dispassion has no love?

Yes. I thought that was why yogis are celibate.
Dispassion tells us that the world is an illusion and not truth. Yogis love God and nature. They try to increase love, and decrease worldly attachments. Being celibate doesn't mean they hate people.

Is there a way to control anger through sadhana?
Hold the breath several times; the anger will go away.

What is the difference between controlling anger and suppressing it?
When you accept it, you control it; when you don't accept, and don't show it, then it's suppressing.

Anger has three forms: hate, hostility, and fear. The root cause of it is attachment. The world would not exist without attachment, and it is present in everyone to a greater or lesser degree.

What do you do with angry energy?
You should dissolve it. As long as you don't accept it, then you can't get rid of it. Anger is a weapon for self-protection. Sometimes we get angry for protection from our own guilt. Jealousy and guilt feelings are part of anger.

So you are not really accepting anger if you still have feelings of guilt and jealousy?
Anger is not a small thing. It comes out with different

faces—resentment, for example. But you think that screaming is the only face of anger.

When I get angry I start to express it and I cry.
That is also a face of anger. You can smile too, and still be angry.

So if a saint has control of desires, then anger and fear will also be controlled?
As soon as fear is gone, the stage called *nirdvandva* (fearlessness) comes. It is the highest stage of a saint.

How can I learn to forgive someone who has hurt me?
It's very hard to forgive someone who has hurt you. The hurt you feel is due to the ego which feels like a loser. The ego never wants to lose. You can forgive someone in a real sense only when your ego accepts that by forgiving the other person you are not losing but winning.

What is the best way to deal with my anger?
Be aware of it. "I am angry." Accept this condition.

You think if I am aware, I won't hit anyone?
That's right. When we are not aware of it, then we go mad.

What if I am still angry after acceptance?
Anger and fear are two sides of the same coin. Why do you become angry? Because you are afraid and want to protect yourself. If you have no fear, you will not be angry.

What about self-pity and grief around anger?
Self-pity and grief are forms of fear.

A bird trapper ties a rolling bar on a long bamboo pole
and pushes it up in a tree near a bird. When the bird
sits on it, the bar rolls over and the bird hangs
upside down. Due to fear the bird clings
to the roller more tightly. While the bird is clinging,
the trapper brings the pole down and captures it.
Even after rolling upside down, the bird
was free to fly away, but in its mind
it was not free.

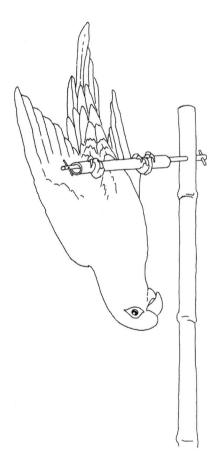

Is working with fear a long term process? What about the present?

When an aspirant wants to stay free from anger, hate, and fear, these demons attach themselves more and sometimes create a kind of madness in the mind. For that, *satsang* is very important. Satsang means association with those who are truth seekers. If you talk about your fear or emotion with someone you trust, gradually it will lessen. If it comes up again, do the same thing. Identify the problem; don't reject it. When you recognize the bush, the bear disappears.

What is fear?
Fear is the other side of anger.
When you accept the fear, you will understand
why you are angry.

How can I plug into the positive energy I know is there?

The flow of energy in the body is blocked when the mind indulges in anger, hatred, and selfishness. Keep your mind pure and you will see how easily the energy moves.

How does one get to feel more confident, to accept oneself more?

We don't accept ourselves when we play the games of others. When we play our own game, standing on our own feet, then we develop confidence.

What is a way to overcome pridefulness?

If you can beg food from your enemy.

And if you can't?
Too proud.

How can I deal with negative effects of the moon or other negative emotions?
Negative emotions can come by negative conditions of the body, such as sickness, or by the environment, or by samskaras. The elements and the environment can be changed easily, but change of samskaras can be very difficult. The moon affects the water element primarily; it can be changed. Cut down on water intake, eat more root foods, and don't sleep during the night of the full moon or the next day. If you're in a bad environment, change the place. To wipe out bad samskaras, you have to do sadhana.

Is happiness peace?
No. In happiness the mind is engaged with the object of happiness, while in peace there is no object, no thought, just peace.

I do sadhana but still feel depressed. Why?
I don't think it's a new thing in human nature to develop sadness and depression. According to yoga, each element predominates for an hour in the body. When either air or ether element predominates it makes sadness and depression, and when earth or water predominates it keeps the mind calm and happy. But those who have attained higher stages in yoga can be helped by air and ether elements. Due to hidden attachments and desires, depression increases. Yoga sadhana can give you the ability to understand what is causing the unhappiness. All yogis pass through the stage of depression, but when their sadhana goes higher they get control over it. Yoga is a very hard path. So when the worldly desires come, don't be disheartened.

Let them come and then remember that desires increase when fulfilled, and die when not fulfilled. You can't fulfill desires forever. Every desire is like a fire; the more fuel you give to it the more it will increase.

What is guilt?
Guilt comes when one realizes that one's actions were wrong, and those unresolved past memories of mistaken actions haunt the mind.

What is the medicine for guilt?
There is only one medicine. Do sadhana and look forward. If you climb a pole you have to look to the top. Guilt is nothing. If we say, "I am feeling guilty," but again repeat the same deed that caused us guilt, then we are using guilt to hide. If we don't repeat, then no need for guilt.

What is guilt? See how long a guilt remains. The feeling of guilt is a good hideout for people who have an inferiority complex. They tell themselves that they feel too guilty to be with others, and by this pretext they separate themselves and enjoy their pain. This becomes a pattern of their life, and in its advanced stage makes them crippled to live in society. The same kind of people also use yoga as a hideout. They live separately and think they are doing yoga, but in fact they don't do yoga—they simply sit in a corner where no one can see them. Forget about your past and your feelings of guilt. Your guilt is all created by your mind, and your mind can also release this feeling. There is no *mantra,* drug, or posture that can cure it. You have to break the pattern by yourself. By talking alone you cannot heal yourself. You will keep on talking, making everything painful. It will never end. You have to break the pattern. Play physical games. Sing and dance.

I understand your
inferiority complex. It can be cured
if you try to get out of it. But most people like
the pain of a thorn in their foot.

Before doing yoga,
you have to make up your mind
that you don't want to live in the confusion
of your thoughts, which cover your mind like a
tangled web of barbed wire.
The next thing is to open yourself by
playing, singing, dancing. In the beginning
people are afraid, but once they come out
of their shells they can do it.
It cures an inferiority
complex very fast.

Where does loneliness come from?
Loneliness comes when you can't be your own friend.
You try to find others to fill that place from outside.
For some time you enjoy their company and the
hidden desire under the loneliness is temporarily
fulfilled. But these desires can't be satisfied for long.
They return, and again loneliness overpowers the
mind. Strive to enjoy loneliness. It will help in yoga.
A prisoner who doesn't care about being released is
able to enjoy prison.

Is loneliness inside of oneself? Does it follow you?
It is a good thing. It is vairagya. Loneliness in its
extreme gives a sense of death, because death is the
only thing which can't be shared with others.

**Sometimes the meaninglessness of everything is
the cause of sadness. How do you deal with it?**
Develop it. It is a dispassionate state of mind which is
very important in yogic life.

How?
Sadness when developed can make the consciousness
very high. But don't develop sadness to attain friends
or the world; that will bring pain.

**How do you deal with this sadness—the feeling
that you have gone nowhere and have no
purpose?**
Accept the meaninglessness of the world and it will
push your consciousness to a higher level.

**What is sadness and what is happiness?
Shouldn't we see God in everything?**
To be able to see God in everybody and everything is
a very high stage. The main thing is to understand the

cause of sadness. Is it a desire for something or a sadness for not having anything?

How can I do the work I do without feeling resentment and frustration?

If you think the burden of the world is on your shoulders then you begin to feel the burden, and in a few years you become hunchbacked. Then one day you realize that the world is existing by itself, and your mind has made it a burden. But the hunchback has already formed. Ninety percent of pain is self-created. You can either accept your duties and responsibilities with a smile or reject them with tears. It doesn't make any difference to the world, but it makes a difference in your contentment.

When we make worldly choices, must we take our feelings into account?

Your choices will depend on how you see things, how you understand, and how you feel. We all see according to our desires. For example, a man was singing devotional songs to God as his beloved; another man passed by and thought he was singing to attract women.

But what does one do about the discrepancy between what one feels and what one understands?

If you really understand, your feelings will agree with your knowledge. If there is a discrepancy, it means you don't know. Feeling comes after knowing.

It's a good practice to listen to and follow the guidance of your heart. It increases will power. But sometimes, when the mind is covered by some attachment or emotion, the guidance can be a delusion.

What happens in crying?

Crying purifies the nerve channels. It takes out excess bile and mucus and strengthens the lungs, but only when a person cries out of positive emotions, not out of anger. There is a *pranayama* that does the same purification for those who can't cry. It is called *ujjayi*. All eight sattvic emotions *(ashta sattvika vikara)* are a natural process for purifying the body. They appear according to the body humor (air, bile, or mucus) predominant in the person. They are described by Prabhudatta Brahmachari as follows:

1) *stambha* (stunned)—body becomes stiff, actionless;

2) *kampa* (trembling)—whole body trembles;

3) *sveda* (sweating)—body sweats profusely;

4) *ashru* (tears)—heart fills with love and tears flow;

5) *svarbhanga* (cracking of voice)—the throat blocks from emotion and one can hardly speak;

6) *baivarna* (change of color)—face becomes pale, flushed, or yellow;

7) *pulaka* (horripilation)—gooseflesh, hair standing on end;

8) *pralaya* (fainting)—the body faints and one loses body consciousness.

These eight changes can appear in any order, according to the element that predominates in the body at the time. If the elements change quickly, then there is a rapid shift from one emotion to another.

RELATIONSHIPS

*Yes, there is one
sadhana for you both, but it is very difficult.
The method is to develop tolerance,
contentment, and compassion.
It needs twenty-four hour awareness.
This is the only way to attain
peace and happiness
in a relationship.*

How does one find a soul mate?
The soul never mates; only the samskaras mate. You can say, "samskara mate."

You know what I mean though.
You don't have to look for it. If you were related in previous lives, you will automatically come together. Samskaras get together like grains of sand falling through a sieve. There is no question of choosing.

Can you achieve realization within a marriage relationship?
Several have attained. Lahiri Mahashaya, Yogananda's guru's guru, is a perfect example of it. He had several children, worked in a government job, and still he achieved a very high state.

Is solitude preferable to being a householder?
No, but a householder sometimes needs solitude to see him or herself from a different angle.

Is a householder's progress slower?
Progress depends upon your honesty. A *sadhu* (renunciate) can be much slower in sadhana than a householder if there is not honesty in sadhana.

Is there a point in solitude where one can transcend personal interaction so that it isn't needed at all?
Individually one can. Sadhus are supposed to do that.

You mean there is another world that exists?
It exists inside you.

Should one limit one's friends and relationships?
Socially you should expand.

Is that important?

Don't consider yourselves sadhus. This creates much confusion. We will talk about the householder level first. After we have talked about householder life, then we can talk about sadhu life.

No one can have everything. We gain something and lose something. In this way life goes on. Without developing the qualities of tolerance, compassion, and contentment we can't live together and can't love each other. A married couple should sacrifice their personal desires and row their boat together. Negativity is not unusual; it exists in everyone. But we have to overpower these negative things by watching ourselves.

When water is poured
into water, both waters become one
and can't be separated.

There is no peace if there is no limitation of desires. We create problems mostly by our own dissatisfactions. No one can be happy all the time. Sometimes we get sad and depressed, and at that time our sadness projects onto the people around us, which creates problems or dissatisfaction. I have not seen any householders who can say that they have no problems. I can't say that householders can eliminate all problems, but they can reduce the emotional strain by understanding the real situation. When a problem arises it becomes complicated by our emotions. If we think about it peacefully, it can be resolved in some way.

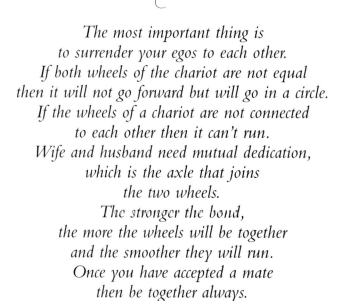

The most important thing is
to surrender your egos to each other.
If both wheels of the chariot are not equal
then it will not go forward but will go in a circle.
If the wheels of a chariot are not connected
to each other then it can't run.
Wife and husband need mutual dedication,
which is the axle that joins
the two wheels.
The stronger the bond,
the more the wheels will be together
and the smoother they will run.
Once you have accepted a mate
then be together always.

From letters . . .

I don't think that any two people can carry on a relationship without taking responsibility for each other for the whole lifetime.

Marriage is very important. Although you live together and you have made a child, still there is a thought in the minds of both of you that you are not married. You can't have the real feeling of oneness until you are married.

You have known your husband for a long time. If you really love him, then you have to tolerate a few of his weaknesses and he has to accept yours. It's a very hard austerity to live with a person. It needs much sacrifice. If you think you will get a better person, then there will be no limit to your dissatisfactions. You will go on searching and you will not find any one hundred percent perfect man. So your whole of life will pass away in pain, and you will feel very lonely. In a few cases it becomes impossible to live together, as when a person goes crazy or develops bad habits like drug addiction or gambling. If people really want to, they can accept, adjust, and live in harmony for the rest of their lives. When old age comes they are a support for each other.

Realization of God depends on devotion and faith in God. If marriage increases these qualities it can help toward realization, but if marriage increases worldly desires it will be a hindrance.

Wife and husband
are like two equal halves of a soybean.
One half alone will not grow.
If the two parts are separated and planted in the earth,
still they will not grow. The bean will grow only
when both parts are covered by one skin,
which makes them
one.

Love and hate are two tendencies of the mind. Because you say in your mind, "I don't love so and so," you feel hate for him. If your mind accepts love for him there will be no problem. It is like self-brainwashing. Your mind is seeking some more exciting man. You find one, and for some time this excitement remains. Then you start to see him as unexciting also. Most couples in America are facing the same problem. The result is: marriage, separation, remarriage, separation. The wheel of life is turning in pleasure and pain, and no peace is ever attained.

Life is full of tides,
like an ocean . . . everyone's boat
goes up and down.

Two people can't live together without sacrificing some of their personal desires. They are free together, but they are not always free individually. If you look into your past relationships, you will find that the separation started when one or both of you started to satisfy personal desires at the expense of the relationship.

Does separation hinder one's inner development? Is it a serious problem for couples to separate?
It depends upon why you marry a person. Is it out of love or simply out of desire? In certain situations, separation can be a tool for growth. Other times separation can mean running away from the problem. Marriage and romance are two different things. When romance is finished, everything looks ugly.

What about duty? Should we desire pleasure and joy, or forget it and just do our duty?
Bearing the burdens of life together peacefully is marriage.

The real reason for the problem between you is not two different sadhanas. The reason could be your ego of being initiated into Tibetan Buddhism and your wanting to pull your wife into it.

Spiritual practice is a personal thing. If you both accept one kind of practice it's okay, and if you don't, still you can each practice in your own way and live together peacefully. There is no reason why a wife who is a doctor can't live with her husband who is a lawyer. They have different trades but it does not interfere with their married life. They can each do their work separately and live together happily.

God is beyond any name and form and yet has all names and all forms. You can worship God in any way. You are worshipping the same God that your wife is worshipping. If God is different in your minds it is an ignorance. God is in your wife. God is in you. God is in your friends. God is everywhere.

By developing tolerance, compassion, and contentment, one can worship God truthfully. If these qualities are not developed, then performing rituals and doing sadhana will not bring any results.

Your egos are not dissolving into each other. One person can't be blamed. Both of you are keeping your egos separate, which makes competition. When a relationship is based on competition you can't live together peacefully.

There is a story of a swan who had two heads.
The swan could eat food much faster than the one-headed
swans. One day the two heads began to argue about
which one ate faster and which one ate slower.
After a heated argument they began to hate each other.
One head found a poisonous berry and said to the other head,
"I can't live with you any longer," and picked up the berry.
The other head said, "Wait, don't eat it! If you eat,
I'll also die." But the first head angrily
swallowed the berry anyway, and thus died
the two-headed swan.

Among ninety percent of householders
this kind of argument is going on,
and then they destroy each other or separate
instead of compromising.

The social duties of a householder are like a weight on my shoulders.

You are free to take another path, a hermit's life for example. But remember no one forced you to get married. You did it through your own desire. So you should do your duties happily.

One can be open, loving, and sharing in all types of relationships—brother, sister, mother, father, husband, friend. To be one with everybody doesn't mean that you should treat your mother and wife the same and have sex with both. They are the same in their true nature but they differ in their relationship to you. When we say "same," we mean you should not hate one person and love another person. "Same" doesn't mean that you have to see their forms the same, their relationship the same. You love your wife and you have a particular bond with her. You love your sister and you have a different kind of bond with her. In this way you relate to all in different ways, but there is one sameness and that is that you don't hate anyone.

Reducing negative qualities and developing positive qualities are not two different things. The monks and nuns in solitude try to control their negative qualities, and when they overcome their negative qualities they come out of solitude. They don't have to try to show love and compassion; the love shines by itself.

What is the difference between divine and personal love?

Divine love is not polluted by desires. Personal love is mixed with desires and attachments.

Can't personal love be divine too?

Personal love minus attachment equals divine love.

Love doesn't come from anywhere. It is already in us. When the mind is purified, then the heart opens up. As long as the mind is not pure then real love can't manifest. But if a person is in the process of purifying the mind, which reduces hate, then love will start growing.

How can we deal with the pain of loving someone who can't accept our love?

You can't force love on someone. If a candle is lit it spreads its light. Pure love will spread by itself. There is no question of acceptance or rejection. If love is mixed with some kind of attachment, it is a different kind of love—it is colored by selfishness, possessiveness, and other desires. In this case rejection will cause pain.

Why do we hang onto fear?

People like the pain of a thorn in the foot. But you haven't disclosed the real problem that is bothering you.

Would expressing it make it go away?

It helps in understanding. When you don't express it, it is like putting ashes on a fire; the fire goes on burning inside.

I could relate twenty-five or more problems but . . .

Separation from a man is causing your pain and uncovering all of your non-acceptances.

How do I learn to accept myself?

You know you can't have a younger body. You can either resist this fact painfully or accept it cheerfully. Cheerfulness is a happiness inside the heart, related to contentment.

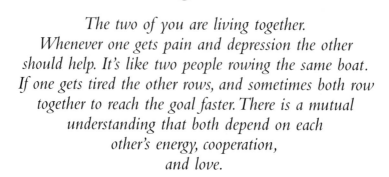

The two of you are living together.
Whenever one gets pain and depression the other
should help. It's like two people rowing the same boat.
If one gets tired the other rows, and sometimes both row
together to reach the goal faster. There is a mutual
understanding that both depend on each
other's energy, cooperation,
and love.

I think of myself as a compassionate and tolerant person, but I am not content.
They are three facets of one thing. A tolerant, compassionate person who is discontent is an impossibility.

I always have a vague anxiety—maybe I'm fearful that my relationship won't last.
When there are many expectations and we don't get those expectations fulfilled we create a feeling of unhappiness. If there is love, and expectations can be kept within a limit, you will see there is no pain or feeling of abandonment.

Many of us seem to be searching for a way to fill emptiness through pleasure.
What is emptiness? You have lost the quality of love so you try to fill the gap. There must be mutual love and a sense of surrender to each other in marriage. Otherwise it will be very painful for both.

Female and male are two energies that need the support of each other. These two energies reinforce each other and grow together. This is the process of Nature. But human consciousness is much higher than that of other beings. Human beings seek a particular type of love in each other, and when they find that love they become one, inseparable. Even the separation of bodies by death can't separate that love. Yoga means union with God. By pure love one can also unite with God. God is everywhere and in everything. If we truly reach out for God in one thing—in love, in art, in devotion, in yoga—then we can reach the real truth.

SEXUALITY

*I have seen people who tried free sex
and they are not happy. I have seen people
who are celibate, and they are not happy either.
I have seen householders living in a
one-to-one relationship; they are unhappy too.
So what is the answer to attain happiness?
The answer is to live by keeping limits
on desires.
It is hard austerity (tapas).
One has to observe strict discipline
made by oneself. One who can do that
can lead a happy life.*

Marriage relationship includes all relationships—parent, child, teacher, student, friend, and lover. If one is in pain the other can help by taking the position of teacher, friend, parent—whatever is needed. This is the beauty of the one-to-one relationship. If these supports are lacking, it is not a real marriage.

You can't share everything with everybody. This is not possible. You are confusing sex with love. Love is a feeling untouched by desires. This love should be the same for everyone.

You cannot compare your having two men with a mother who has two babies, because that is a different kind of relationship. It's the same kind of argument as, "A man's wife is a woman, and his mother is also a woman, so what's the harm of his having sex with his mother?" I can't agree with such arguments.

I am not telling you to change your desires. But I'll say that there is no end to desire. A person who is in the habit of eating varieties of food always remains unsatisfied. There is no contentment. Even though the person eats food and enjoys it, still the person craves some new thing. There is no limit, and if the desires are not limited, there will be no peace. If parents are not in peace the children will get their samskaras, and then their lives will become painful when they begin to understand the world.

In marriage it is difficult if one partner wishes to be celibate and the other does not. You both have to decide about it. I believe sex is a sacred part of love and can't be shared with everybody. The wife/husband relationship is right for sharing sex because they have taken a vow to be one.

The marriage relationship is not only physical. It is a relationship of pure love. You sacrifice your personal desires to maintain your love and your relationship. Marital sex is not a physical thing. It is a very important part of love. It should be considered as sacred as love for God. If a person wishes only to fulfill sensual desires with another person, then it doesn't matter with whom he or she lives. It's not love.

It is always upsetting for a woman to see her husband with other women. Also, if a man is honest, it is upsetting for him if his wife goes to other men. If wife and husband agree to be free to have sex with others, they may not get upset, but they don't have pure love for each other. They simply live together but they are not as one, spiritually and emotionally. It is the reason that ages ago wise people made a rule of one-to-one relationship.

A woman who loves her husband can't and shouldn't tolerate her husband having sex with any other woman. A saint once sang a song which means, "The lane of love is so narrow that only two can walk at a time."

No one can have peace if sensual desires are not put under a limit. The family system is for limiting sensual desires. If the one-to-one relationship is rejected, then the mind will always search for new relationships, and this desire will never end. Some day the old body will be incapable of fulfilling sensual desires, but the mind will be full of desires. This is the greatest pain in life. A mind full of sensual desires doesn't accept aging. This non-acceptance creates much pain in old people. They die in pain and develop samskaras of pain due to not being capable of fulfilling desires.

*The best thing for attaining peace is to
keep the desires within a limit and accept yourself.
Accept the marriage relationship.
Accept old age, and accept death. This acceptance
will stop new samskaras from forming.
There will be contentment in life,
and contentment is peace,
love, God.*

Yes, men relate to women with sex desire. Also women relate to men with the same thought. There is no end to it. The more a person gives freedom to sex desire, the more it comes. And then what happens? Like a deer running after a mirage, one dies of thirst. Those men who relate to you with sex desire relate to other women in the same way, so their desire jumps from one woman to another woman to another woman. When they get old the body can become incapable of enjoying sex, but the desire still jumps. This is the worst pain in life.

Brachmacharya is a very big word. One who is on the path of *Brahman* (God) is a *brahmachari*. Its main purpose is to control desire and retain semen *(bindu),* which is a very powerful energy. Married people who limit their sexual desires are brahmacharis.

In ancient times all saints were householders. They would have children, and also they would do yoga. But in their minds only yoga was real and reproduction was a play of nature.

Is sexual continence necessary for sadhana?
Is the purpose of it to preserve one's semen?
Semen (bindu) is vital energy. In its purest form it is called *ojas*. This ojas has tremendous power and can go straight up to the top of *sahasrara*. A person who is moderate in sexual behavior is also a brahmachari.

What is moderate behavior?
The male and female sexual act is natural once a month. If this is reduced even more it is better for sadhana. When people think about sex a lot, they get more trapped. Sex can also be used as a method of yoga, if it is not on the physical level.

It's difficult to attain sexual dispassion. To center on a higher level while engaging in sex seems contradictory.

It's very difficult. Sex is one of the natural tendencies. It can be transcended or eliminated gradually. Practice very slowly. Otherwise the mind will revolt.

What if the mind is in the habit of revolting?

Try to set limits step by step.

What is the role of sex in spiritual life?

Kundalini is sex energy. When its flow is toward the world *(pravritti,* evolution) it is called sex desire, and when its flow is upward *(nivritti,* involution) it is called awakening of kundalini, which opens the energy centers and ultimately brings enlightenment. The physical sensations as it flows in either direction are the same. So when kundalini is vibrated, any one of many emotions, including sex desire, may arise. At this point a person should not be afraid of sexual desire, but should simply watch it.

In *tantric* yoga, the method is to use sex as a means of controlling the flow of the energy. But certain tantric practices are dangerous. The danger comes when the aspirant of *tantra* forgets the aim of attaining liberation and gets addicted to sensual pleasures. Normally a person should keep to a middle path, which can also open up the energy centers.

What is the middle path?

Moderate sex. Once a month is yogic moderation for married people.

Doesn't sex also generate energy?

Yes, it generates and makes a child.

Is brahmacharya the same for men and women? What about loss of fluid?

Semen is energy in both sexes; fluid is its gross form. The rules are the same for men and women. Women also have semen which is called *raja*.

Is it possible to control sexual sensation through mantra?

Not mantra, but mind.

How is abstinence different from brahmacharya? What does yoga do to change that energy? What practices transmute sexual energy?

What is important is preserving semen as a vital fluid. Celibacy doesn't mean abstaining from sex; the desire for sex must be transcended. If one is trying to stop and still gets thoughts of sex, that is only natural. There are specific practices to preserve semen. Pranayama is the best method. A few *asanas* are also for that. But a person can be enlightened without brahmacharya if sex is lived in a natural way. Don't mix the sadhu trip in this thing, because there are different rules for sadhus. People read books, then try to follow rules and go crazy. Those rules are for hermits.

Maybe it depends on how you are happiest?

What is happiness? Follow simple rules and don't go to extremes.

Psychology talks about sex repression and its bad effects.

What is not sex? Our energies are passing from one person to another right here. No two of us have the same energy. But when we are together it passes naturally. According to tantra, brahmacharya is not abandonment of sex but transcendence of it.

Is there an evolutionary reason for increased sex in our culture?

The more the mind is developed, the more it will search for sensual pleasures. You have sexual freedom, but people are still searching for more pleasure. They are experimenting with different ways, and still they are discontent. This discontentment leads to violence and sexual perversion.

If you get pleasure by discharging semen, you can get several times more pleasure by storing semen. It's not easy, but also it's not impossible. The best way is to gradually reduce the loss of semen.

If you fall from the top of a tree or from the top of a rock there is no difference—you will get hurt either way. Losing semen by homosexuality, heterosexuality, or masturbation is the same, because the loss of semen is the same. Time is going and not coming. Every second of your life is going. Your life will get shorter whether you do good things or bad things. But if you do good things, you will gain good things—like happiness, peace, bliss. If you do bad things, you will gain bad things—like anger, hate, jealousy, fear. In both cases loss of life is inevitable, but the attainment is different. For example, two travelers go to Mount Shasta. One goes singing, playing, and enjoying nature, while the other goes quarreling with people, being angry and afraid. Both reach Mount Shasta, but one's heart blooms like a lotus and the other's heart is dark like a prison.

Sexual perversion develops due to fear. When a person can't relate to another on the sexual level without fear, the mind naturally develops perversion.

Society doesn't accept homosexuality for various reasons. The union of male and female is natural for reproduction. As it is considered natural, the social structure is based on this union. If the whole country becomes homosexual, then what will be the shape of society? Society has discouraged homosexuality because of the fear that it will destroy the structure. This discouragement creates a guilt feeling in homosexuals. If you want to stop it, then don't do it. If you want to do it, then don't feel guilty about it.

Do you know that in the months of February and March, September and October, when the sun changes its position, emotions increase and people develop craziness, anger, and increased sex desire? By doing regular sadhana one can keep the mind in balance.

Pregnancy

During pregnancy
a woman should avoid hard
physical labor, physical discomfort,
indulgences in grief, fright, and so forth.
As soon as a woman conceives,
her attachment to the baby begins.
This attachment creates a feeling
of protection for the fetus
she is carrying.

A newborn baby is the purest form of a human being.
This purity remains until the baby understands
me/mine, you/yours.

Does a couple's consciousness at the time of conception determine the consciousness of the child?

The child gets some of the samskaras of the parents.

How does that affect the child?

If the parents have anger or hate at the time, the child will get those samskaras. If they are in a higher, loving space the child will have a more loving nature.

Is it okay for a woman to get pregnant if she knows she won't be living with the father?

What do you think?

I don't know. I am confused about it.

For a child, male energy is very important.

I don't know how to undo the harm of negative emotions that I put on my unborn child.

First, don't worry yourself by thinking of the negative things you have done. Do positive things now.

How do negative emotions affect the unborn child?

After three to four months, the fetus develops emotions and can feel the negative or positive emotions of the mother.

Does the parent's negativity have permanent effects on the child?

It makes a print on the mind of the unborn child—makes a tendency in the child to behave in a certain way, which can be permanent.

How will a child, or anyone, overcome them?

By giving the child love. You have to understand the cause, and then put positive things into the mind.

What about abortion?

It is killing. But when you control the death rate, then you have to control the birth rate.

Is birth control bad?

No, but self control is better than birth control.

It's harder!

Nothing is easy.

Chinese say the soul enters the child two hours after birth. What do they say in India?

Twenty-two days after conception. Life is already there but the soul enters in twenty-two days. The emotions and the mind develop after four months.

One takes birth in the world by one's own samskaras. The parents also pass on their samskaras, and then all kinds of samskaras—those of friends, relatives, and society—fill the child. It's like filling an empty bag with all kinds of garbage. But one is capable of emptying the bag at any age in life. It is also a samskara to want to get rid of that garbage. No one can remain like a newborn baby—free of the influences and samskaras acquired through living in the world.
In the first month of pregnancy the five elements

(earth, water, fire, air, and ether) become condensed into a mass by the three humors—mucus, bile, and air. From the second to third month the head, arms, and legs begin to sprout. In the fourth month the emotional heart, the seat of consciousness, develops. [This is not the physical heart which appears in the first weeks.] So from the fourth month a baby develops desires of taste, smell, and touch, which manifest through the desires of its mother. At that time if the mother's desires are not satisfied it can affect the growth of the child.

In the fifth month the mind (*manas*) develops and the soul wakes up from its subconscious sleep. In the sixth month intellect (*buddhi*) comes in. The baby develops its full shape. In the womb the baby feels pain and discomfort, but it's all like a dream.

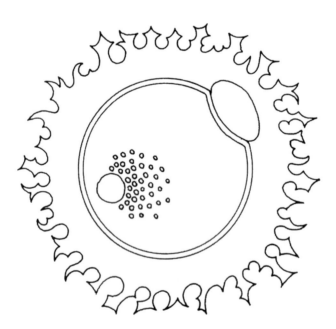

Read scriptures and stories
about saints. This is also a sadhana.
It makes good samskaras in the mind of a baby.
After the fourth month a pregnant woman is conscious
of two hearts—her own heart and the baby's heart.
Her awareness is directly connected
with the baby inside her womb.
This relationship of mother and child
is the highest of all physical
relationships.

You don't need to worry
about whether a child feels pain or pleasure
inside the womb, because it's the law of nature that
everyone must pass through those stages.
God has made a system of nature in
which everything is balanced.
If suffering comes, then a strength
to tolerate it also comes.
If a child in the womb suffers certain kinds of pain,
then some kind of pranic energy definitely
develops which gives the strength
of tolerance.

According to the law of nature there is no choice about having or not having children. We have adopted an unnatural life, so we can say, "I'll have children," or "I don't want to have children."

The world is overpopulated, it's true, but a couple can replace themselves by making two children. In this way the population will always remain the same. If both male and female agree not to have babies and live like hermits, that's another thing. But from a biological point of view your desire to have a baby is natural, and your husband should respect your desire.

The desire for reproduction is mainly in the female, which is natural. Your desire to have a baby is a reality of your body and your nature. The sexual union of male and female is for reproduction. If you and your husband are attached to each other, what difference will it make if you are attached to your own seed also?

Nature is a huge machine. It is so perfect that it maintains a balance of births and deaths. Earthquakes, floods, famines, diseases, and even wars are natural means of controlling the population. If the earth is over-filled with living beings, then something will happen and the population will reduce. It doesn't make any difference if a part of the earth drowns in the ocean; somewhere a new earth will come up when it is needed. In the same way, if a person doesn't want to have children, then someone else will give birth in twos, threes, or fours.

God's creation is also God. So everything is God. Worship creation, admire the beauty of it, and be happy.

Your depression, sadness,
pain are part of your pregnancy.
Even though you had an abortion, still the
full effect of the pregnancy is not gone.
Pregnancy is not only physical; it is emotionally
connected with the subtle body.
That is why the mother develops love
for the baby,
even if it is not born.

PARENTING

Children copy their parents,
friends, and teachers. They will develop
the habits of the people around them.
So if you want your child
to be honest, peaceful, and happy
you should be that way
first.

Can you say something about right attitude with children?

Become a child. If you love them it's easy. You were and are a child. A tree grows from a seed and the tree never separates from the seed. We don't have to pretend to be a child; that nature is always in us.

What's the most important thing to teach children?

We learn by using our senses. So the most important thing to teach children is to use their senses properly—to really hear, look, touch, smell, and taste. One who has learned this can attain any worldly knowledge easily.

In handling my child, I don't know when to give in and when to discipline.

There is a difference in age and energy between a child and an adult. Parents should always keep this difference in mind. Because they don't scream, run, and jump like children, parents can't tolerate children running and jumping, and they use anger to try to stop them. When children's energy is stopped by force they develop frustration and rebel against their parents. So parents need to learn to set limits and rules without anger, and to allow children time and place to run and play.

Children should play together, and if your children learn something bad then explain to them that it is not good. They will believe you, if you are honest with them.

Can you speak about duty of children to their parents?

Children's duty is to copy the parents.

What is parent's duty to children?

To take care of them. If you take good care, they will copy you.

Is it ever the duty of children to care for the parents?

It's their duty if they learned it from their parents. If you take care of your mother, your daughter will take care of you.

What do you think of the commandment to honor thy father and mother?

They are the first gurus (teachers).

I teach small children in school, and sometimes I worry about competition. It seems bad for them.

Competition that hurts others by thoughts, actions, or words should not be encouraged. Competition is bad when it causes the children who lose to develop fear. On the other hand, competition encourages children to develop their physical and mental strength. Competition is fun for children. If there is competition between two groups, then one child will not have to take the entire responsibility for losing and will not develop fear. The members of the groups should be changed regularly so that they will not develop a feeling of group identity. You should not worry about competition, but take care to encourage both sides equally.

Doesn't parenthood create attachment? Is that good?

Attachment is necessary for the needs of nature, for survival of the species. But dispassion can also arise from the relationship. Caring for children as a selfless service can cultivate the qualities of tolerance, compassion, and contentment, which can also bring dispassion. For example, a father is attached to his son and his son yells at him. In that moment if the father sees clearly that his son can't bring him peace, then at once he can get dispassion.

Did you say householders must have attachments?
With understanding. I am attached to this chalkboard. I'll not cry if it breaks, but I'll keep it safe. Householders can't say, "I'm unattached," and let their children play in the street and get killed by a car.

Can parents be less attached when children are older?
Your duty changes; that changes the nature of your attachment.

Can you be more explicit about how duty changes?
You don't treat your sixteen-year-old daughter like a child.

It is hard to know when I am doing my duty and when I am treating her like a child.
That is attachment without understanding.

How young can a child be to read scriptures with understanding?
It depends on the child's samskaras. Some can understand from an early age; some can't. They can understand through the actions of the parents. Reading a book is not important. You can explain things in your own language. You don't need to quote scriptures.

How do you know what is your duty when disciplining a child? When do you spank, and so on?

Discipline yourself first and the child will come around. The child is your mirror. Spanking a child is like training an animal to do as you say without understanding why. The best thing is to help children understand what is right and what is wrong. But you have to understand your own emotions first.

If you, yourself, act out your anger and other emotions with your child, how can the child understand what is wrong?

Why do parents disapprove of a spiritual leader? Why do they want their child to come to them instead of to a leader?

It's a fear of losing control of a child.

Children are pure; can we keep them that way?

No, the world pollutes.

Are young children established in witness-consciousness?

As long as they don't recognize the world.

How do you teach children to meditate?

Meditate yourself, and they will copy you.

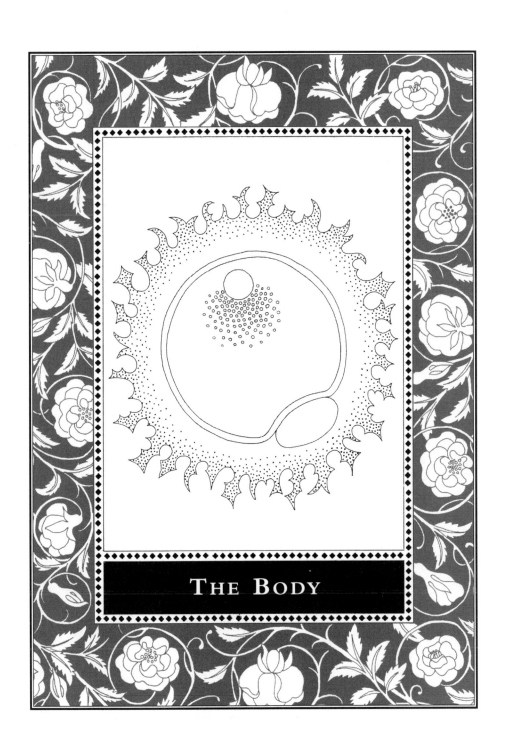

THE BODY

DIET

Eating doesn't need to be complicated.
A sattvic diet is balanced and consists of food
you can easily digest. Rules are made
only when food is plentiful;
in times of famine
one eats what one can get.

For yoga *sadhana* a balanced diet of vegetables, grains, fruits, nuts, and milk is best. We don't want food that is inertia-producing *(tamasic)*—like meat, fish, decayed or stale food, as this disturbs the mind. We eat mainly energy-creating *(rajasic)* and pure *(sattvic)* foods. Milk is life—it is the first food given by God, and it is classified as sattvic. It causes mucus, but mucus balances the burning quality of bile. Mucus is a very important part of the body. A diet too high in mucus, however, creates laziness, sex desire, and overeating. In the winter season bile increases to keep the body warm and strengthen the digestion. Mucus-type foods prevent the increased bile from burning the stomach and intestines. For cold countries, fat-producing food is important. During summer when it is hot one can live on a fruit diet.

Is physical sadhana affected by diet?
According to Ayurveda (classical Indian medicine), human bodies are classified into three categories or humors: air humor predominant, bile humor predominant, and mucus humor predominant. Food is also classified in this way. The food we eat is assimilated differently by each of the three different body types. If one is air predominant, that person must eat food that reduces air (gas). Suppose one has a weak earth element. Grains, which are predominantly earth element and mucus producing, will help this person. The idea is to maintain an equilibrium of the three humors.

All the five elements exist in our bodies in a certain ratio; when the ideal measure of any of these elements is increased or decreased, the result is sickness. Yoga methods are also classified into three categories: heating, cooling, and moderate. A person who is mucus predominant (cool) will need heating methods. So sadhana and diet are both related to a person's predominant body humor. If all three are perfectly in tune one will feel wonderful and sadhana will go very well.

Where does sugar and a craving for it come in?
Sweets are mucus predominant and they decrease bile and air humors. If a person craves them, the body is out of balance. However, when one begins doing *pranayama* (breath control), bile increases; then the body needs more sweets or cooling foods.

What are bile foods that aren't meat?
Eggplant, green leafy vegetables, yogurt.

How do the three *gunas* relate to the five elements, and the three humors?
All living forms are made of a mixture of the five elements *(tattvas),* and all elements are alive. Different kinds of forms with different kinds of qualities *(gunas)* are created by the relative mixtures of elements. *Tamas guna* is related to earth and water elements and mucus humor; *rajas guna* to fire element and bile humor; *sattva guna* to ether and air elements and air humor. In this way everything is classified according to the five elements, three gunas, and three humors.

Is coldness mucus predominant?
Mucus itself is cold. Mucus predominant people can stand more cold.

Does doing yoga cause food to be assimilated more easily?
It enables the body to extract more from the food taken in.

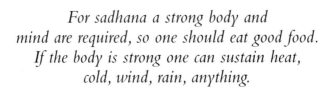

For sadhana a strong body and
mind are required, so one should eat good food.
If the body is strong one can sustain heat,
cold, wind, rain, anything.

Don't make too many rules about food;
just eat a simple, pure diet,
and forget about it.

Is there a certain diet for pranayama?

Pranayama is very heating. When one does a lot of it one should eat cooling foods: wheat, rice, corn, milk, *ghee* (clarified butter), sugar, garbanzo, cucumbers, figs, roots, fruits.

During the full moon, pressure builds up in my head. What can I do about it?

Fast, by taking one meal a day for four days of earth-predominant foods. Best are those that grow under the ground. Also, take less water.

Is it possible to live with no food?

It's not impossible; some *sadhus* do it.

What about a nun in Europe who drank no water?

There was also one woman saint in India who lived without food and water. It's possible to develop the ability to extract life force from the air. In *samadhi,* sadhus do not eat for thirty to forty days and they still remain healthy.

How often and how long should one fast?

Once a week rests the digestive system (from after dinner one night until dinner the next night). Medicine is needed according to the sickness; if you don't need fasting, don't do it for long periods. If the body is really impure, then do a three to nine-day fast with hot lemon water to drink. There are several methods.

It's a good practice to go on a fruit diet for a week or a month, or to go on a liquid diet. It helps very much in purifying the body.

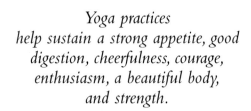

*Yoga practices
help sustain a strong appetite, good
digestion, cheerfulness, courage,
enthusiasm, a beautiful body,
and strength.*

What is the role of diet in consciousness?
If the diet is easy to digest and doesn't create too much heat or cold, it is good for the mind and body.

Why don't yogis eat meat?
Some do. If they live in Tibet, they have to eat meat to survive. But we get meat by killing. If we can live without killing it is better.

Does the violence of killing pass into you when you eat meat?
The animal doesn't want to be killed. In eating meat you eat the animal's attachment to its body which remains in the meat.

My teacher eats meat; would you ever eat meat?
If it grows on trees.

It's been proven that plants have feelings too. Isn't it just as bad to eat them?
When you break a green plant it feels pain, but when leaves, fruits, and flowers mature they are replaced as part of their natural cycle. Also, vegetable consciousness is different from animal consciousness.

I know I'm attached to the body, but I try all sorts of diets. I don't know whether I'm mucus predominant, or what I am. I don't know what to eat!
Eat what you can digest. If you think about food too much it becomes a trap. Some people eat raw food. That is good, but if you can't digest it, then it is bad for you. It can't be classified as a sattvic diet for you.

Is it best to eat just two meals a day?
Yes.

What is the best time space between meals?
Eat before noon and after sunset, approximately eight hours between meals.

One shouldn't eat between meals? I've heard that it's best to eat small amounts continually.
For what purpose? If it's for health it's all right. For yoga, if you eat two meals then your digestive system will work just twice and you can get enough time for sadhana.

I never felt I had interest in food until I decided to improve my diet. Now I think about food all the time!
Eat good food and don't think about it.

I work around food and find myself eating all day long. How can I change?
Put a limit on your eating—two meals a day. A person can develop the eating habits of a goat! Mind makes the habit; mind can break it.

Do you in your own diet try to avoid chemicals, additives, pesticides, and so on?
I don't know about those things. I eat what I get. Eating doesn't need to be complicated. A sattvic diet is balanced and consists of food you can easily digest. Rules are made only when food is plentiful; in times of famine one eats what one can get.

What are the effects on the body of ginger root and cayenne? Some think they are a kind of "speed."
They are bile predominant and heating. Ginger root reduces mucus, but long usage will dry up the system. Cayenne is a blood purifier and is good for the eyes.

How about ginseng?

It's a Chinese herb, bile predominant. I've experienced that it is good for the nerves and heart.

What spices can be used in a sattvic diet?

Spices are used in such a way as to balance each other. For example, turmeric with coriander, cinnamon with nutmeg, black pepper with anise seed. Garlic, onions, and asafaoetida (hing) are strong and hard to digest. Although garlic heals wounds and strengthens lungs, it is heating and is not good for meditation.

Isn't it better to avoid all spices?

Spices are not very important. A healthy person can digest anything.

Does standing on the head help digestion? If so, when should it be done?

It helps. Do it after *asanas,* or after meditation, but not after taking food.

How long should one stand on the head?

Up to five minutes, and gradually the time can be increased to twenty minutes.

SLEEP

Habit of sleeping so much
is difficult to break.
You are taught to sleep more.
Once you develop the habit of less sleep,
it will not be difficult. But it needs practice.
Take light food at night.
The sheep herders in the Himalayas
walk all night and sleep very little
in the morning.
It is natural for them.

Are there any rules for sleeping? Is one position better than another?

The best position is on the left side with the right knee pulled up. This keeps the right nostril clear, which helps to keep the body warm. [*Pingala,* the heating breath, flows through the right nostril. *Ida,* the cooling breath, flows through the left nostril.]

Can you comment on how much sleep people need? I find that five hours are not enough.

It depends on the food you eat and your physical activities. Generally, from age thirteen to twenty, eight hours are needed; after twenty, six hours are enough for most people. Sleep from 10:00 p.m. to 4:00 a.m.

Can it be broken up? Sleep, wake up at dawn, do *sadhana,* then sleep again?

One could do it that way. Early morning, before the distractions of the day, is the best time for sadhana, especially concentration on inner sound (*nada*).

Is it true that more than six hours of sleep creates lethargy?

When food is well digested, then you don't need much sleep. Your body will be active and full of energy.

I'm trying to sleep six hours, and I'm having a hard time.

You can do it. It's a matter of practice. Once you develop the habit, you will have no difficulty. Take light food at night.

DRUGS

Hallucinogenic drugs
are not good for yoga sadhana.
To get out of illusion one needs a pure mind
free from all delusion.
If you take a drug and create more
delusions, then how can you
get out of illusion?

Can we reach the same level of awareness alone, as with *ganja* and other drugs?
By yoga you can attain much higher levels. Drugs merely excite the energy centers *(chakras)* and can give you a glimpse of what it looks like.

Are there harmful effects from mixing ganja and pranayama?
It brings craziness. *Ganja* and pranayama can't go together. Pranayamas are for increasing *pranic* energy. If smoke goes in, it will harm pranic energy.

Do you recommend that we don't smoke ganja? If so, why?
Ganja is an addiction, just like tobacco and other drugs. All addictions are harmful.

Why do sadhus smoke it in India?
The reason is that they don't want to face the world; they don't have to. They try to finish sexual desire by using ganja and turning their minds away from it.

But sometimes it is sexually stimulating.
In the beginning it is, but its regular use for many years causes impotence.

A lot of my friends and I smoke it regularly. It's kind of a social thing. Everyone I know smokes ganja.
So . . . ?

Is there any truth to the theory that drugs make holes in the aura and reverse the polarity of the body?
No holes. I don't know about the polarity theory. I know very simple things.

*According to Ayurveda,
marijuana (ganja) is classified as one of the
mind-sharpening herbs, but it is used as a medicine.
If it is used in bigger doses for a long time it can
cause loss of memory and impotence.
I knew several siddhas (highly advanced yogis)
who used it, but they were not householders;
they had no responsibilities.
It becomes addicting after some time,
and addiction to anything
is a trap.*

It's a general feeling among older people that all those who do yoga are drug people.
It's a wrong idea. Drugs and yoga don't go together. No one sits in the dirt while wearing clean pants.

How about LSD? It has given spiritual insight to many westerners.
I don't think LSD is good for sadhana. It accelerates the change of elements inside the body a hundred times more than usual, which causes visions of different kinds of geometrical patterns, colors, lights, and so on. LSD can harm any nerve in the brain permanently.

Sometimes I see patterns of movement. What are they?
They are caused by the cycling of the five elements—earth, water, fire, air, and ether. Every hour the elements make a full cycle, each one predominant for a different length of time. Each element has a colored geometric form which can be seen. Earth is characterized by a yellow square, water by a white crescent, fire by a red triangle, air by a blue star, ether by a white circle. When these change, patterns are created and they make designs. LSD causes the patterns to change faster than normal. When one takes LSD, one sees the patterns, but can't fix upon one element. Concentration cannot be maintained and so one doesn't get the power of the patterns that are seen.

Friends of mine used to sniff glue and they said that it makes the ears ring very loudly. Was that *nada* (subtle sound)?
Nada means any sound, but yoga is concerned with the nada which appears due to purified nerve channels. The kind of intoxication you mentioned

pollutes nerves. These impure nerves get excited, vibrate, and make sounds. It's not helpful to listen to that kind of sound.

I've heard that one can hear the electrical nervous system during meditation. Is that nada?
Yes. In meditation the movement of *prana* (vital energy) gets very clear. It also happens when one is in a high emotional state. One should be very still and concentrate. Nada intoxicates if one concentrates deeply on it.

Swooning the mind by nada
and swooning the mind by drugs
are two different things.
The swooning stage is the same, but the results
are different. One intoxication brings
knowledge and the other
brings depression.
When the mind is intoxicated by nada it feels
very light, peaceful, and it doesn't want
to indulge in worldly things.
This state is also called
dispassion.

Can't drugs be helpful in acquiring knowledge of the Self?
Then all here would be enlightened!

HEALING

The body is not only for enjoying the world;
we need the body as an instrument
to worship God.
If this is our aim, then
we should try to keep the body fit.
The physical body is the main instrument
for doing sadhana. If it is well,
then sadhana goes well.

Is there a system of healing or medicine which is superior?
Each culture has its own methods, and people have faith in them. *Mantra* can cure a cobra bite if faith in the mantra is strong enough.

Both Ramakrishna and Ramana Maharshi suffered from cancer. They took medicines, but it didn't mean that they were afraid of pain or death. Yogis accept God's program. If they get sick they will take medicine, but if they are dying they will not worry about it.

Does one pray and ask God to help?
Either accept the sickness, or pray to God to relieve you of the *samskara*.

In healing does one interfere with the cosmic plan?
Yes.

Is that interference also a part of the plan?
Yes, it just extends the time factor of one's life.

What about Christ's healing miracles—were they real?
Yes, they were real, but still all of those people died.

Why are some born with physical or mental handicaps?
There are many reasons: unhealthy environment, hereditary diseases, bad samskaras, or even good samskaras. Sometimes a saint needs just one more birth to finish all samskaras. That birth might take place in a handicapped body. In this way no more samskaras are made.

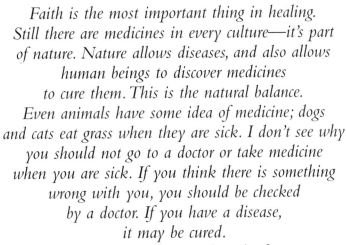

Faith is the most important thing in healing.
Still there are medicines in every culture—it's part
of nature. Nature allows diseases, and also allows
human beings to discover medicines
to cure them. This is the natural balance.
Even animals have some idea of medicine; dogs
and cats eat grass when they are sick. I don't see why
you should not go to a doctor or take medicine
when you are sick. If you think there is something
wrong with you, you should be checked
by a doctor. If you have a disease,
it may be cured.
If there is no disease, then the fear
inside your mind will go away,
and automatically you will
become stronger.

How does one discriminate when being kept alive by machines? Doesn't this interfere too much with the cosmic plan?

The person will die anyway. No amount of modern technology can save us from death. It is scientific ego at work.

If a sickness is God's wish,
then taking medicine is also God's wish.
Nature cures the sickness of those
who have complete faith.

Do you feel pain?

If I say no, you'll hit me with a rock! I feel pain. *[shows hip and finger which were injured in a game]* It's a body function; all feelings are there, but the difference is how attached we are to pain.

What can we do to save the planet?

First, we should understand how we are damaging the planet. The air, water, and earth are being polluted by human beings. Smoke and poisonous gases are polluting the air, and waste materials are polluting the water. Cutting down trees, cutting into mountains, and overpopulation are destroying the earth. To save the planet we have to learn to live in natural ways.

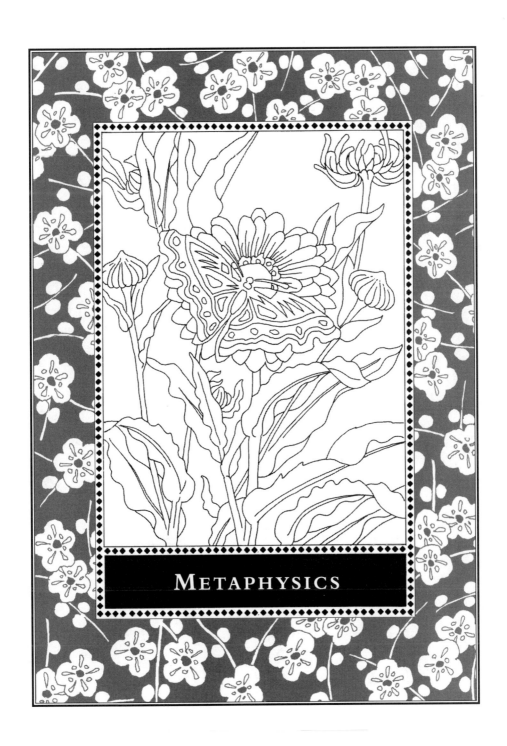

METAPHYSICS

METAPHYSICS

In the beginning there was God
in the form of sound. That sound is Om,
represented by the symbol ॐ.
Om is the sound of God, the sound of creation, the
sound of liberation. Om is composed of three Sanskrit
letters (अ), (ऊ), (म), which
stand for the three gunas: (अ) represents rajas,
(ऊ) represents sattva, and (म) represents tamas.
In Hindu cosmology these energies
are identified with three aspects of God: Brahma,
the creator; Vishnu, the preserver;
and Shiva, the destroyer.

Two eternal energies, *Purusha* and *Prakriti,* are the cause of the manifest universe. Purusha is the Principle of Consciousness that pervades all animate and inanimate things. Prakriti, when manifest, is Nature itself.

Nature is a force both inside and outside of us that governs everything. Nature is made up of three qualities, or *gunas*—*sattva, rajas,* and *tamas.* Before evolution begins, the gunas are in a state of equilibrium in *mula prakriti,* which is an energy center located in the center of *sahasrara chakra* at the top of the head. Sattva guna is light, purity, and balance; rajas is passion, action; tamas is inertia, ignorance, and destruction. The source of the three gunas is God *(Brahman),* so everything is controlled by God.

The three gunas evolve into creation, and are manifested in the macrocosm and microcosm as three "bodies": causal, subtle, and gross. In the beginning there is only pure consciousness, which is expressed by sattva guna. When rajas guna (action) and tamas guna (destructive energy) overpower this pure consciousness, sattva guna changes into *maya* (illusion), or the universe. This is the cause of creation, so it is called the causal body. Then, in another burst of energy, rajas and tamas again overpower sattva, and *avidya,* a state of ignorance, is created.

In avidya the three gunas act to create the subtle body, which is composed of seventeen energies. Sattva first creates the intellect *(buddhi),* which has discriminative power. Rajas next creates the ego *(ahamkara),* and the ego unfolds into evolutes according to the three gunas. *Sattvic* ego produces the mind *(manas),* the five subtle senses *(jñanendriyas),* and the five subtle organs of action *(karmendriyas)*. At the same time, *tamasic* ego creates the five subtle elements *(tanmatras)* as the objects of the senses. Now the subtle body is complete.

As tamas increases, the gross elements *(bhutas)* evolve from the subtle elements. These are space, air, fire, water, and earth. From these elements the gross body and all gross forms evolve. In this way, the three bodies—causal, subtle, and gross—are formed.

The subtle body is sometimes referred to as the astral body. It is a very pure form. Due to the life force of *prana,* the subtle body exists beyond the life and death of the physical body, and so it has access to the impressions *(samskaras)* of present and past births, the desires and experiences of pleasure and pain.

Pleasure and pain occur when ignorance,
tamas guna, is predominant. Happiness occurs when
creative energy, rajas guna, is predominant.
Bliss occurs when pure consciousness,
sattva guna, is predominant.

We measure the difference of life forces existing in various forms by our senses, but some life forces are beyond the capabilities of our senses. To measure these we must use instruments, such as the microscope or telescope. When we see the tiniest animal made of a single cell, we see it is complete in itself. It eats, reproduces, and so on. This means it has the power of consciousness (mind), which is called *jñana shakti;* it has action, which is called *kriya shakti;* it has matter, which is called *karma shakti*. These three *shaktis* in one are called *para shakti,* which is God.

In Hindu scriptures it is said, "God walks without legs, God works without hands, God eats without mouth." This little animal is the same. It has no limbs, but it does everything without limbs. If our means of measurement were unlimited and we could see more deeply inside this single-celled animal, who knows— we might see that the whole universe is there.

No one can remain in the same mood all of the time. Within every hour the predominance of each of the five elements changes in the body; and, according to the predominant element, the emotions and thought waves *(vrittis)* also change. Every two hours the predominant guna changes. Because of this continuing cycle of the elements and the gunas, a person can't stay in one emotion for a long time.

Yet even though we feel ourselves swinging from depression to happiness, still the overall balance of elements and gunas remains the same. Each person is a miniature form of the universe, and the same changing cycles repeat in the universe, but in a larger framework. In this way the universe has been going on for an indefinite period of time.

I was reading in Sri Isha Upanishad that this universe is finite like a coconut; beyond that is the spiritual sky.
There are seven sheaths to the universe. Everything we see—stars, planets, earth—is within the first sheath.

What is beyond the seventh sheath?
It's called *loka lok,* or *shunya* (void), or God.

Could a spacecraft get to loka lok?
If it doesn't dissolve.

Into different substances?
Different temperatures, forces of gravity, gases. But we have not yet even fully discovered the human body.

Is loka lok inside the body?
It's the Self.

So you don't need a spaceship.
[Nods]

Do we decide to evolve?
It's human nature. It's also the nature of the universe. Evolution is called *pravritti;* energy flows down and out, expanding and multiplying. The reverse condition, involution, is called *nivritti;* all energy is withdrawn from the world of objects and is pulled back to its source.

There is a theory that we are an experiment begun long ago by beings from another planet.
You can also make a theory.

Is pravritti the stage on the cosmic clock where we experience pleasure and pain?
That is pravritti; now wind it up. Act like circus people, who go to a town and spread out their world (pravritti), and then gather it up (nivritti). It takes time, but it is still nivritti.

How does one know when one's pravritti is done?
The mind gets a sense, if one has the right samskaras. If not, pravritti is limitless.

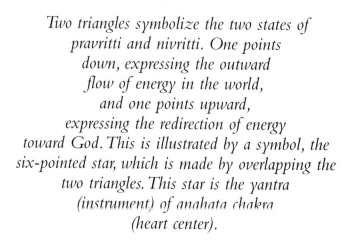

*Two triangles symbolize the two states of
pravritti and nivritti. One points
down, expressing the outward
flow of energy in the world,
and one points upward,
expressing the redirection of energy
toward God. This is illustrated by a symbol, the
six-pointed star, which is made by overlapping the
two triangles. This star is the yantra
(instrument) of anahata chakra
(heart center).*

In the fifth verse of the *Bhagavad Purana* there is a description of the creation of the universe. It shakes me. Is there any way to understand it besides literally?

Read it in a yogic way: What is *sumeru?* It is the "tenth door" or mula prakriti, the center of sahasrara chakra in the crown of the head. Suppose you are a planet. You have seven chakras, which are *lokas,* or universes; seven oceans around each loka; seven *patalas,* nether regions. Around each energy center in your body there are blood vessels; this liquid equals the oceans. When you understand it is yourself, then you can apply it to the creation outside.

People say the earth plane is all maya. Is there reality here?

Maya is real as a dream is real. When you awake, the dream is gone.

What remains then?

Truth. The veil over truth is maya.

Are we affected by the planets? If so, how?

Sun, moon, earth, and other planets are all inside of you. Everything outside is a projection of inside. Just as outer planets affect this earth, in the same way each individual is also affected by the energies of different planets. According to astrology, when someone takes birth one planet predominates. The planets are always moving, so turn by turn each planet's energy predominates and affects us accordingly.

Does meditation affect the influence the planets have on us?

Since meditation can change the threefold *karma,* it can have an effect in other ways also.

I don't understand how the universe can all fit inside of a person.
A magnifying glass is so little, but it can make things so big.

Is the universe itself a being?
Yes, just as inside you there are many life forms, and yet you are one being.

Are the *chakras* like solar systems?
The chakras are called lokas (universes).

What chakra are people mostly in?
All chakras—no one can stay in one state of consciousness, except one who is in the immortal stage and can control the elements.

How about *muladhara chakra* (at the base of the spine)?
There are four kinds of bliss in the first chakra. We need all four: material bliss, sensual bliss, spiritual bliss, and the bliss of wisdom. The first chakra is a reflection of the top chakra (sahasrara chakra).

So the universe can play any game with us. Does everyone have a role to play in the universe?
Your desire is your world. Every person's world is different. We each play our own game with our own desires, and that is our world.

If all is one, what is bad?
We don't see all as one, and that is bad.

How does the moon affect one?
The moon affects according to its phase because of its pull on the water element.

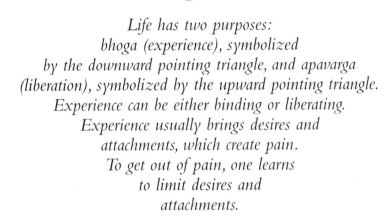

Life has two purposes:
bhoga (experience), symbolized
by the downward pointing triangle, and apavarga
(liberation), symbolized by the upward pointing triangle.
Experience can be either binding or liberating.
Experience usually brings desires and
attachments, which create pain.
To get out of pain, one learns
to limit desires and
attachments.

What is the difference between a person and a star?

Each person is complete, so each is a star. That is the beauty of God. Everyone is so perfect.

I find myself in a cycle of being in the here and now, and then another cycle comes when I'm never here now.

This is caused by the change of elements. The moon affects this change and causes a person to be off balance for several days. There is a method to cure it: plug the right nostril with cotton at sunrise and keep it closed until sunset on those days.

I feel this is a physical answer to a metaphysical question.

The breath is not just physical; it works on the subtle body. Changing the breath will change the whole cycle of elements in the body. The elements control all thoughts, emotions, actions.

Should one always close the right nostril?

It is normal to have the left nostril open at sunrise, but it gets unbalanced.

What is *kundalini*?

Kundalini is the energy of Nature that is left over after the gunas have evolved into creation. In the physical body, it is a storehouse of energy at the base of the spine, and it is generally dormant. During meditation, when the mind becomes quiet and the thought waves become very shallow, subtle energy blocks are removed. At that time kundalini energy can awaken and begin to move up. This stage creates a kind of pleasure that turns to happiness, and then to bliss in its later stages.

Its real name is *kula kundalini*. Kula means body; kundalini means winding. Anger, hate, jealousy—all bad habits are wound up in the body. When those negative qualities are reduced, the awakening of kundalini begins. When negative qualities are completely wiped out, liberation is achieved.

I've heard kundalini is dangerous—that it can kill us.

Kundalini energy can be excited by yoga, dreams, accidents, drugs, shock, or sometimes by illness. If this energy is excited and one is not able to handle it, one can be harmed physically and mentally or be trapped in worldly desires.

Kundalini is female. A man has the ego of masculinity so he feels the femininity of kundalini. If he can imagine that God is masculine, and that all of us— men and women—are feminine lovers of God, then his ego of masculinity will disappear and he won't be lost in sex desire. This was the attitude of Ramakrishna Paramahansa.

If one can awaken kundalini by drugs, why do yoga? Wouldn't drugs be faster?

If you take a drug you can get trapped—energy goes up and comes down hard. If you really try to excite the energy, you can do it; but the method, time, place, and dosage must be right. Only by regular *sadhana* (spiritual practice) can one move the energy up with permanent benefits.

Is awakening of kundalini necessary for enlightenment?

Yes. A being is bound by six *vikaras* (impediments)— existence, birth, growth, change, decay, and destruction.

When certain symptoms appear in the physical body, such as sensations of light and sound, we say kundalini is awakening. With this awakening, the chain of vikaras is broken.

Is it possible for the kundalini to go up and down?

Yes. It goes up and down until it pierces *shri chakra* (in the sahasrara complex) and the non-dual stage is attained. Then it stays stable.

What is aura?

Vyana prana (one of the five primary subtle energies) spreads throughout the body and extends out around the body for four fingers' width. We can all see it and feel it if we try. In meditation this aura can fill the room. Some yogis in jungles appear like balls of light at night.

Is there a maximum limit to which the human aura can extend?

If a person has a strong will, the aura can extend very far.

In an enlightened being, could it go for miles?

It can. When Hairakhan Baba first appeared in the Hairakhan jungle, he was seen like a star from twelve miles away.

People say a pyramid works; some tests show it's not so.

If it is correctly made, it can work.

What is it that works?

It reverses the triangle of pravritti, which means the loss of energy is stopped.

Are there times when the pyramid manifests more energy than other times?

The full moon, new moon, and changes of planets affect it just as they affect *mandalas.*

Are there teachers on subtle planes helping us?

The world is a teacher. In the same way all other planes are teachers. To attain a subtle plane we need to develop higher consciousness by doing our sadhana with faith and devotion.

Are there spirits from other realms who can give truth through a medium?

I only believe in Self.

What is the significance of the number 108?

The number 108 is a multiple of the number 9, which is the highest numeral. In the Sanskrit alphabet there are 54 letters, from "a" to "ksha," which when doubled for once ascending and once descending equal 108. So a *mala* (rosary) has 108 beads.

In one minute we inhale and exhale 15 times, and in twelve hours 10,800 times. In doing *japa* for 10,800, a mala of 108 beads will be rotated 100 times.

The number 9 is the highest number. The number 108 adds up to 9 (numerologically, by adding the individual numerals together). All multiples of 9 also add up to 9. It is a number that doesn't change.

The number 9 is considered auspicious. That is why the *Gayatri Mantra* has 27 syllables (2 + 7 = 9). In the Hindu scriptures there are 18 major *Puranas* and 18 minor *Puranas.* There are 18,000 verses in the *Bhagavat.* There are 18 chapters in the *Bhagavad Gita* and 18

chapters in the *Mahabharata*. The battle of the
Mahabharata lasted for 18 days.

The total number of years in each *yuga* adds up to 9:

> *Sat yuga* = 1,728,000 years = 18 = 9
> *Treta yuga* = 1,296,000 years = 18 = 9
> *Dvapar yuga* = 864,000 years = 18 = 9
> *Kali yuga* = 432,000 years = 9

> all four yugas total 4,320,000 years = 9

There is a triangular-shaped space defined by three
points in the head. The path of *sushumna nadi* goes
from *mula* in sahasrara, to *ajña chakra* in the forehead,
to *mastaka granthi* (head knot) at the base of the skull.
We generally inhale 21,600 times daily. If, by yoga
methods, we can reduce that number to 108 breaths,
the prana stays within that triangle. At this stage, one is
completely enlightened.

**I've read that we're now in kali yuga. What does
that mean, and what is the next stage we will go
into?**
There are four yugas, and each yuga is divided into
four parts. After the fourth, or kali yuga, there is
complete destruction.

Is kali yuga the beginning or the end?
In a circle you can't say what's beginning and what's
end.

**Can you tell us some of the characteristics of
kali yuga?**
Kalah, the root word of kali, means "quarrel" or
tamasic vrittis. Kali yuga has one-fourth truth.

What's the other three-fourths?
Ignorance.

How long do the yugas last?
Enormous periods of time in one sense, but in another sense they can also be finished by our own efforts. There are four yugas (cosmic ages) with a duration ratio of 4:3:2:1. The first, sat yuga, lasts four times as long as the last, kali yuga. 432,000 is the length of time in years of the kali yuga, which is going on at present. 432,000 times two equals 864,000 years, the length of dvapar yuga; 432,000 times three equals 1,296,000 years, the length of treta yuga; and 432,000 times four equals 1,728,000 years, the length of sat yuga.

In sat yuga, *dharma* (the law of truth) is perfect.

In treta yuga, dharma is three-fourths predominant and *adharma* (ignorance) is one-fourth.

In dvapar yuga, dharma is one-half predominant and adharma is one-half.

In kali yuga, dharma is one-fourth and adharma is three-fourths predominant.

The total of four yugas, 4,320,000 years, makes one cycle which is called *maha yuga*. The cycle of yugas also exists in the individual body, as it progresses toward death, and in the collective body of humankind.

After completion of one cycle, creation is destroyed, but its samskaras stay at rest in seed form. This rest between cycles is called *maha pralaya*. Sometimes *khanda pralaya* (partial suspense) prevails and part of the universe disappears, as in the drowning of a continent, natural disasters, accidents, disease. For example, one person's sickness is khanda pralaya in the maha yuga of that person's life; death is maha pralaya for that person.

The four stages, dharma to adharma, as represented by the yugas, are also present in the same ratio within each yuga. At the present time we are living in the second stage (more or less) of kali yuga, which is tamas guna predominant, causing quarrels, depression, ego, and so on. But an individual person can get out of this cycle by sadhana.

LIFE & DEATH

KARMA

Karma is action. It is cause and effect.
There is no uncaused action
nor is there any action
without effect.

Karma is of three types:

1) *samchit* (collected)—the unfinished mass of actions of past births, both good and bad, which are yet to be worked out and appear in this birth in the form of desires;

2) *prarabdha* (destined)—the result of karma already worked out in a previous life which appears in the present life in the form of fate;

3) *agami* (present)—the karma we are continually making in our present actions, which will influence our future actions.

How do we get rid of karma of the future?
When present and past karmas are conquered, there will be no future karmas. Good actions wipe out past karmas and then future karma will automatically be good because there will be no bad tendencies remaining to pull you toward bad actions.

Is it possible to reach a stage where you are no longer creating karma? If you do your actions for your *guru* (teacher), do you get karma?
What kind of actions?

Helping others; following your guru's advice.
Then you are collecting good karma. It is quite clear that doing good creates good karma. But you should be aware that helping the poor or unfortunate is good only for your *samskaras;* you can't change the samskaras of others.

How is karma different from samskaras?
Karmas are actions we perform with our body, mind,

and senses. These actions create imprints in the mind. The mental imprints created by our actions are called samskaras. Samskaras then become the cause of our actions in the future. Sometimes the term karma is used for samskara.

Does the guru take on the disciple's karma?
Can you eat for your baby? The person who is waiting for the guru to take away karma will remain waiting. One should take full responsibility for one's karmas and work on them.

Does an enlightened being still have karma?
Yes. The existence of such a being is karma, but in this stage actions don't make imprints for a future life.

What constitutes non-karmic activity?
Non-karmic activity occurs when a person totally surrenders the ego of being a doer. To ignore the sense of "I am this body" is hard work, because you are still active; the heart beats and the mind acts. But you are not the body. When this becomes clear to you, then you will work and at the same time not create karma. Your body will function by reflex action.

What is destiny?
Destiny is the result of samskaras, or tendencies, which are created by past and present karmic actions. Everything that happens is within the law of cause and effect (karma). We can avoid certain karma by intelligence, but even intelligence is within karma.

Do we have control of destiny through God within us or through mind control?
You have control up to the limit of your mind. If you touch fire it will burn. Don't blame destiny for it.

*It's most important to
be aware of our actions all of the time.*

SAMSKARAS

Samskaras are the impressions

in the mind from earlier actions, or conditioning.

According to this theory, one carries the prints

of actions from earlier births.

The purpose of each lifetime is to live out

the samskaras created in the previous lifetimes.

At the same time, actions in this life

are creating new samskaras.

In this way samskaras exist layer upon layer.

The layers can be peeled off by meditation or by

spiritual life. Samadhi is one way by which

samskaras can be wiped out completely,

and this leads to liberation.

Are samskaras "original sin?"

Samskaras are good and bad both. You may become successful by your samskaras, and you may become a gambler.

So good actions can bind us just as bad actions?

Any action binds. One binds with an iron chain, the other with a gold chain.

How can good actions be binding?

If you become president by good actions, still you are not free.

Is it attachment?

Yes.

How do we get bad habits?

We get good and bad habits from two types of samskaras (impressions): those formed by actions in past lives, and those formed by actions in our present life. It is very difficult to have any control over habits from past life samskaras unless we develop strong will power by doing hard austerities *(tapas)*. Our present life samskaras begin from the time we are babies in the womb and are receiving the emotions of the mother. These habits are not as difficult to break. As soon as we understand that they are wrong we can stop them. But bad habits which are formed by past life samskaras are very dangerous. For example, a person loves gambling. In a future life the person becomes addicted to gambling. It gives pleasure and cannot be stopped because it is guided by past life samskaras. By continued gambling more samskaras are built, and in this way the person's life degenerates.

Good and bad samskaras are like seeds
of different plants kept in a bottle:
some grow in winter, some in summer,
and some in the rainy season.
If we throw all the seeds
on the earth, the seeds which grow in
that season will grow and the others will remain
dormant. Exactly the same thing happens with
samskaras. All kinds of samskaras are in us
but they grow according to the people, places,
or things with which we associate.
If we associate with depraved people,
the bad samskaras will automatically sprout
and good samskaras will remain dormant.
If we associate with truthful people,
samskaras of truthfulness will
automatically come up.

How do we eliminate the effects of past deeds?

The effects of past deeds are called samskaras. They are eliminated in two ways: by attaining *samadhi*, and by cultivating good qualities—contentment, compassion, tolerance, and so on.

By striving for and attaining these qualities, do we gain enlightenment?

Attaining enlightenment and wiping out samskaras are the same thing. As soon as the veil is taken away, you are there.

What happens if enlightenment is not attained and samskaras are not removed in this life?

You will begin in the next life where you end in this one. You cannot lose if you try.

Even high saints have samskaras and act according to them: just as Rama was sent to the jungle and separated from his wife, as Krishna was separated from his *gopis* and fought battles, as Buddha left his palace and faced so much pain and suffering, and as Jesus was crucified.

Can we work out our own samskaras, or do we need the help of someone else?

You have to work out your samskaras by yourself. Help comes by itself from time to time.

How can we keep from forming more samskaras in daily living?

Work in the world like a bank teller who works all day with money but doesn't own it. The teller won't cry if the money is stolen, but the owner of the bank will. If you can keep yourself unattached like the bank teller then you won't create bad samskaras.

What is good and bad? Aren't they the same?
On one level there is no good and bad, but as long as you have that question, you are on the level of good and bad.

The world is an abstract art. We all see in it what we want to see. There is a mixture of good and bad, and both are important for making the wheel of nature turn. There can't be day if there is no night. For some, day is good; and for some, night is good. The main thing is to make the present peaceful. Forget the past and don't think about the future. The future is based on the present. If the present is peaceful, then gradually the future will be peaceful.

A human being
is not entirely trapped by samskaras.
It is possible to weaken negative samskaras
and cultivate positive ones.
Otherwise it would be useless to try
to attain enlightenment.

DEATH

One who takes birth will die.
In other words,
one takes birth to die.
Death is sure and is always waiting.
Because we don't know when
we will die it is said, "Death
comes from behind."

Is where we go in dreams similar to where we go at death?
Life is also a dream, and death is the end of that dream. After death another dream starts.

Is it true that life is a preparation for death?
Yes, it's true.

Do we experience many spiritual deaths in a lifetime?
What is spiritual death?

Death of ego and attachment?
That is death of illusion; spirit doesn't die.

What can I do to overcome my fear of death?
Attachment to the body causes fear of death. It is the strongest attachment. Even a newborn infant has this attachment. To overcome the fear of death it is necessary to accept that we all have to die. No one can save us from death. It is easy to say, "That person will die," but we are afraid to face our own death. Fear disappears gradually as bodily attachment decreases.

Is all spiritual work done on the physical plane, or on some other planes?
All three planes (gross, subtle, and causal) are together.

Why do we fear death?
Ignorance. We don't understand what death really is. Why are we afraid on a dark night? Because we can't see.

Some fear seems to be conditioned into us.
It has been developing from the first time the individual being *(jiva)* died.

Life's essence is absolute, omnipresent,
and immortal. Death is but a change of form.
Human beings, animals, the vegetable kingdom,
the mineral kingdom—all are alive.
They take birth, grow, decay, and die (change form).
When one form changes into another form it is called
death, although the life force still exists in that form.
For example, as soon as a plant dies,
a second life force takes birth and starts
to decay it. When it is completely decayed,
a third life force starts working.
This cycle of change of forms
goes on and on, but the essence
of life is always there—
it is immortal.

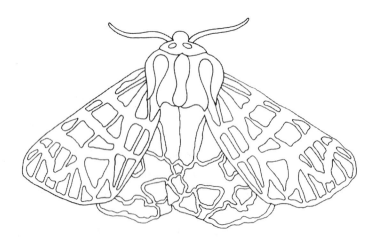

No one can change the world's cycle. A jiva will take birth, grow old, and die. But by developing faith one can be saved from fear of the future, fear of death. The jiva accepts that the responsibility is God's.

It's hard for me to work in an old people's home. It makes me feel terrible.
Why?

Everybody is dying.
So . . . ?

It's so unattractive.
It is also attractive. If you try to understand death, it can take away the fear of death. You can develop dispassion.

I feel repulsion.
If no one wanted to work with old people then what would happen to them?

I identify with their pain. That's what is so bad.
You identify with the fear of death. You don't want to accept that you also will go through the same process.

How can one help a dying person who has anger and fear?
It's very difficult for a person to accept death. That person has fear, and fear creates anger . . . no fear, no anger.

Is that fear of bodily death or fear of the ego dying?
We relate death to the body. Body and ego are always together.

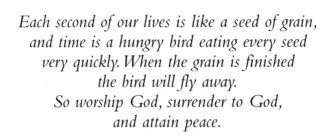

Each second of our lives is like a seed of grain,
and time is a hungry bird eating every seed
very quickly. When the grain is finished
the bird will fly away.
So worship God, surrender to God,
and attain peace.

Everyone has a fear of death. Everyone is attached to illusion. Everyone is afraid of salvation because no one wants to leave this world. If God comes and says, "I'll give you salvation if you are ready to die," you will see that not even one percent will choose salvation. When you arrive at a thoughtless stage in meditation your attachment to this world comes up in the form of fear and tells you, "Come back, come back!" When Buddha was in deep meditation all such things would come and disturb his concentration. The deeper you go in meditation the more these ghosts come. But if your aim is true these ghosts can't pull you down. You will understand that worldly pleasures are not real.

You wrote me about the death of your friend.
Everybody takes birth to die.
Every moment is reducing our life.
Some are dead, some are dying, and some will die.
No one will be saved from death. A pitcher breaks
but the air inside the pitcher doesn't break.
The body dies, but not the Self (atman).
He was your friend and he is still your friend.
Forget his body and your attachment
to his body.
His atman is alive.

What is the fear of rebirth?
Rebirth means we have to die. There is no fear of rebirth, but fear of death.

The idea of going through this life again is dreadful!
That happens when a wife and husband fight.

Will samadhi give complete understanding of death?
For a person who attains samadhi, death becomes like replacing an old coat with a new one.

From letters . . .

Your daughter was killed, and you know that she won't come again, and no one can bring her back. So the question should be erased from the mind. The aim of life is to attain peace and bliss; in other words, God or truth. Now if you keep your mind busy thinking about the past events of family affairs, then you are sowing the seeds of thoughts, which will make many branches, leaves, and fruits. You should know that freedom from thoughts is bliss, and that is salvation. If you want to be in peace then cut the tree of thoughts that is growing inside your mind, and don't sow the seeds of new thoughts. You are your own doctor. Forget the outer world, keep your mind free from past events, and you will get salvation.

REBIRTH

Ego makes desire; desire makes rebirth.
We are reborn to fulfill our desires,
and in fulfilling them
we make more samskaras.

How do you interpret reincarnation?
You mean rebirth? First understand what death is: complete forgetfulness of past identities is death. When memory is regained, that is reincarnation; when it is not regained, that is rebirth. In Christianity there is no rebirth; in Hinduism there is no death. They are both true—the body never takes rebirth and *atman* never dies.

I have out of the body experiences which are new to me.
They are new because you don't know your past lives. When we have forgotten our past lives, every second is new.

Does it mean anything to have forgotten our past lives?
It is nature's law.

Is it too mind blowing to be aware of all lives?
Memory is blocked for the purposes of *pravritti;* otherwise creation would stop. The universe is created, and there is a natural balance to keep it going on. How it keeps in balance is beyond our mind. At times it seems that bad overpowers good, that there is more pain than pleasure, and so forth. But if we take a long view we can see the balance.

How does remembering past lives happen?
All actions are already inside us from many past births. Only an eighth of our mind works, and the rest is in a dormant stage. When the dormant mind is awakened one remembers all past lives, just as if one saw them on TV. It can happen by yoga practice, or by faith and devotion. You can't know of past incarnations until you attain higher samadhi.

The higher you get, the better your memory gets, but also you supposedly get more dispassion. What's the purpose of the memory?

As consciousness gets higher, samskaras get thinner and one can see the past. It's consciousness, not the memory, that gets higher; the memory is incidental.

So the process of remembering past lives is like untying a knot, and others who tell you about past lives don't know?

What is the proof? You must do it by yourself.

Is it important to know what your last incarnation was?

How can you say it's not your imagination? It is important to eat the mangos and not to count the trees. The important thing is to find out about the present life, then the past will be known by itself.

Do we release samskaras through knowledge of past lives?

Knowledge of past lives can show you the root of your samskaras and you can dig it out, but knowledge of past lives is not easy to attain. Some are born with the ability to know, but they are only one in a million, and this ability is easily lost by indulging in the world. For others, knowledge of past lives comes by attaining samadhi.

Are past lives important—to know about them, I mean?

Past lives always count, but no one can prove past life knowledge to others. Only by ourselves can we learn that the past, present, and future are all one. An honest seeker of the truth doesn't waste time in trying to understand theories, but accepts the influence of karma and samskaras, and tries hard to change them. The shore is not far for those who do not stop swimming.

How can I come to realize what is said about reincarnation? It's not part of my life experience.
Without getting samadhi, you can't experience it. Without silencing the mind, you can't get samadhi.

Is everyone reborn and do we get a second chance if enlightenment is not attained?
Rebirth is caused by desires, by the confused mind. If one had no desires then one wouldn't be reborn. A person dies in confusion, takes birth in confusion, and lives in confusion. This illusion keeps one from knowing who one was, who one is, and who one will be. When this confusion becomes less dense, one begins to understand who one was and who one is. Yoga *sadhana* is one way to get out of this confusion.

If it's desire that makes rebirth, can't we just desire not to be reborn?
What is the strength of that desire? A dog can be a human being if desire for it is strong enough. But you know, a well-fed dog let loose still digs in the garbage pile.

Is this an endless process? Is rebirth ever over?
There are several cycles. You shoot up from one to another.

But you remain an entity, just larger and more aware?
[Nods] This cycle never ends. Some day you can be a planet and again make circles around the sun.

Do you believe in Christ's coming in the second millennium?
Higher beings come from time to time. The name and form is not important.

Do higher beings come with a purpose?
Their appearance itself is a purpose.

Is Christ going to come again in the body?
He can come again at any time. He doesn't need any special body. Any body can become Christ.

Is there a specific number of souls in the universe?
If you put one hundred cups of water in the sun, you will see one hundred suns. The cups can be reduced or increased, but one sun always exists.

One who identifies with the body dies
because the body dies;
one who identifies with the soul
is immortal.

APPENDICES

GLOSSARY

adharma: ignorance; non-truth; opposite of truth

agami: karma we make in our present actions

aham Brahman: "I am God," a phrase of Self-affirmation which is repeated as a discipline of yoga

ahamkara: one of the four minds; ego, the faculty of the mind which identifies with the world

ahimsa: nonviolence; one of the five yamas (restraints)

ajapa: automatic repetition; a method of tuning mind and mantra with breath

ajña chakra: energy center located between the eyebrows; the seat of one's own inner teacher; often called the third eye center

ajñana: wrong knowledge; a state of ignorance in which one identifies the world as real

anahata chakra: energy center in the spine located at the level of the heart, often called the heart chakra

anantam: infinity

aparigraha: non-hoarding; one of the five yamas

apavarga: liberation; one of the two purposes of life

asana: posture; third limb of ashtanga yoga

ashanshakti: freedom from attachment; fifth of seven stages in spiritual practice

ashram: home, or living quarters, for a group of people with similar spiritual goals

ashru: tears; one of eight purifying emotions

ashta sattvika vikara: eight purifying emotions—stiffness, weeping, sweating, trembling, change of color, cracking of voice, horripilation, fainting

ashtanga yoga: eight-limbed yoga; a comprehensive system of yoga which combines disciplines for the body, breath, mind, and spirit

asteya: non-stealing; one of the five yamas

atma vichara: the practice of Self-inquiry—"Who am I?"

atman: the higher Self; soul; energy of God in a being

aum, or **om:** primordial sound of creation, the sound of God

avidya: ignorance

Ayurveda: classical Indian medical science

Babaji: Sanskrit title of respect, reverence

baivarna: change of color; one of the eight purifying emotions

Bhagavad Gita: Hindu scripture in which Krishna explains karma yoga, bhakti yoga, and jñana yoga

Bhagavad Purana: Hindu scripture relating stories about Krishna

Bhagavat: Hindu scripture relating to Vishnu and Krishna

bhakti yoga: spiritual path of devotion, worship

bhava pratyaya: born with supernatural powers as a result of samadhi in a past life

bhoga: experience; one of the two purposes of life

bhutas: the five gross elements—space, air, fire, water, earth

bindu: center point of chakras where energy is concentrated; seed; semen

Brahma: God, as creator

brahmachari: lit. "one who walks on God's path"; one who limits sexual desire

brahmacharya: continence; one of the five yamas

Brahman: absolute God

Buddha: the founder of Buddhism; a saint born in 568 B.C. in a kingly family in India, on the border of Nepal

buddhi: one of the four minds; intellect; the discriminating faculty of the mind

causal body: one of three "bodies," represented in the macrocosm and microcosm

Chaitanya Mahaprabhu: a saint of bhakti yoga, who lived from 1407 to 1455

chakras: energy centers distributed along the spinal column and in the head

chitta: one of the four minds; consciousness; memory; the highest of the four minds, into which all the others must merge before liberation is possible

darshan: spiritual audience

deva: god

dharana: concentration; sixth limb of ashtanga yoga

dharma: the law of truth; righteousness

dhyana: meditation; seventh limb of ashtanga yoga

dhyana yoga: spiritual path of meditation

dvapar yuga: the third of four yugas; the age of one-half truth

ganja: marijuana

Gayatri mantra: a sacred Sanskrit mantra of 27 syllables

ghee: clarified butter

gopi: cow girl; devotee of Krishna

gross body: one of three "bodies," represented in the macrocosm and microcosm

guna: essential quality; everything in the universe is composed of the three essential qualities—sattva, rajas, and tamas gunas

guru: teacher; in yoga, the spiritual teacher

guru maharaj: title of great respect for a spiritual teacher

Hairakhan Baba: an Indian saint who first appeared in the Hairakhan jungle, believed to be one of the immortals

ham–sah: mantra for ajapa pranayama, meaning "I am That"

hatha yoga: seven step system, which includes shat karma, asana, pranayama, pratyahara, mudra, meditation, and samadhi

ida: subtle nerve (nadi) related to the breath, flowing through the left nostril

Ishvara pranidhana: surrender to God; one of the five niyamas (observances)

jagrat bhumi: first three stages of spiritual attainment, where a yogi knows the difference between the individual being and God

japa: repetition of God's name or a mantra

jiva: individual being; soul

jñana: highest knowledge; knowledge of the subtle elements

jñana shakti: power of consciousness

jñana yoga: spiritual path of intellectual processes, knowledge

jñanam: knowledge

jñanendriyas: the five subtle senses; the "idea" of smelling, tasting, hearing, seeing, feeling

kaivalya: supreme dispassion

kalah: lit. "quarrel"; root from which kali is derived

Kali: Hindu goddess

kali yuga: the fourth of four yugas; age of one-quarter truth; our present time

kampa: trembling; one of the eight purifying emotions

karma: action; the law of cause and effect

karma shakti: power of matter

karma yoga: spiritual path of selfless action (service); all work is done for God, without expecting reward

karmendriyas: the five subtle organs of action; the consciousness of feet, hands, tongue, genitals, and anus

karmic: anglicized adjective of karma

khanda pralaya: partial rest, or suspense

kirtan: call-and-response chanting

Krishna: incarnation of Vishnu, in dvapar yuga

kriya shakti: power of action

ksha: one of three combined consonants at the end of the Sanskrit alphabet

kula kundalini: the actual term for kundalini; lit. "body winding"

kundalini: a storehouse of energy at the base of the spine, by which a yogi transcends the body and the world

kundalini yoga: spiritual path of subtle energies and chakras

Lahiri Mahasaya: a householder saint who died in 1895; Yogananda's guru's guru

laya yoga: spiritual path of dissolving the mind into superconsciousness

loka: realm, or universe; everything within our physical universe is considered to be in bhu loka, or the lowest of seven realms

loka lok: highest of seven realms; also called shunya

madhyama nada: first stage of inner sound, the "unstruck" sound, emanating from the heart chakra

Mahabharata: Hindu scripture in which yogic life is explained in a story of war between two kingly families—the Kauravas and the Pandavas

maha pralaya: the great rest between cycles of yugas

maharaj: Sanskrit title of respect; lit. "great king"

maha yuga: lit. "great cycle;" a period comprising all four yugas together, or 4,320,000 years

mala: a string of 108 beads, used for repetition of mantra (japa); rosary

manas: one of the four minds; the faculty of the mind that records sense impressions

mandala: a two or three dimensional design that can be read; used to invoke divine energies; a tantric language

mantra: syllable, word, or phrase that has power due to its sound vibration; sound that activates energy centers

mantra yoga: spiritual path of sound vibration

mastaka granthi: lit. "head knot," at the base of the skull; one of three knots in the body that must be broken through to achieve liberation

mauna: the practice of silence; self-discipline of not speaking

maya: illusion; God's manifestation as the world

Mount Kailash: mountain located in eastern Tibet, believed to confer merit upon pilgrims who walk around its base.

mudra: lit. "seal" or "lock"; posture or gesture practiced to awaken and direct kundalini upward

mula: the center of sahasrara chakra in the crown of the head

muladhara chakra: energy center at the base of the spine, where the latent power of kundalini is stored until awakened

mula prakriti: source of all creation, in which the gunas reside in a state of equilibrium before evolution

nada: subtle, inner sound

nada yoga: spiritual path of inner sound vibration; discipline of concentrating on the subtle sound

nadi: subtle nerve channel

nirdvandva: state of complete fearlessness; highest stage of a saint

nivritti: involution; the drawing in and directing upward of energy toward the realization of Self; the reverse of pravritti

niyama: observances; the second limb of ashtanga yoga

ojas: subtle electrical energy in the body; purified form of semen and raja

om, or **aum:** the primordial sound of creation, the sound of God

padarthabhavani: non-perception of external world; sixth stage of spiritual practice

Pandava: the virtuous kingly family in the *Mahabharata*

para nada: highest stage of inner sound, emanating from muladhara chakra

parama siddha: one who has attained the highest knowledge

para shakti: power of God; combination of jñana shakti, kriya shakti, and karma shakti

Parvati: Shiva's wife

pashyanti nada: second stage of subtle inner sound, which emanates from svadhishthana chakra as light

patala: nether region

Patanjali: sage of approx. 200 B.C. who systematized the practices of Yoga; author of *The Yoga Sutras*

pingala: subtle nerve (nadi) related to the breath flowing through the right nostril

Prabhudatta Brahmachari: author of *Chaitanya Charitawali*

Prakriti: the principle of manifest creation; Nature itself

pralaya: fainting; one of the eight purifying emotions

prana: vital energy; life force

pranayama: control of prana, breath; fourth limb of ashtanga yoga

pranic: anglicized adjective of prana

prarabdha: fate; result of karma which was worked out in a past life and is bearing its fruit in the present

pratyahara: turning the mind inward; fifth limb of ashtanga yoga

pravritti: evolution; the flowing downward and spreading out of creative energy; opposite of nivritti

pulaka: horripilation; gooseflesh; hair standing on end; one of the eight purifying emotions

Puranas: ancient Hindu religious stories

Purusha: the principle of consciousness that pervades the universe

raja: subtle sexual energy in women; the female equivalent of semen

raja yoga: spiritual path of eight parts; also called ashtanga yoga

rajas guna: one of three essential qualities; the quality of passion, action, creation

rajasic: anglicized adjective of rajas guna

Rama: incarnation of Vishnu, in the treta yuga

Ramakrishna Paramahansa: great nineteenth century saint of Bengal, India

Ramana Maharshi: great Indian saint who lived from 1879 to 1950

Ramayana: Hindu scripture in which yogic life is explained in the story of Prince Rama

sadhana: spiritual practice

sadhu: renunciate; monk; one who has taken religious vows; sadhvi is a female renunciate

sahasrara chakra: energy center in the crown of the head; thousand petal lotus

samadhi: superconsciousness; eighth limb of ashtanga yoga

samchit: karma of the past, yet to be worked out

samskara: impressions or imprints in the mind, created by our actions

samata: equality; seeing everything and everyone as equal

samprajñata samadhi: lower stage of superconsciousness

samyama: a stage when dharana, dhyana, and samadhi are perfected and practiced together

sandhi: grammatical rules of elision in Sanskrit, through which letters change by preceding or following other letters

santosha: contentment; one of the five niyamas

satsang: lit. "union of truth"; association with truth seekers

sattva guna: one of three essential qualities; the quality of balance, light, purity

sattvic: anglicized adjective of sattva guna

sat guru: spiritual teacher who is a Self-realized being

sat yuga: the first of four yugas; age of perfect truth

satvapatti: experience of truth; fourth of seven stages in spiritual practice

satya: truthfulness; one of the five yamas

satyam: truth

shabda: sound

shakti: power, energy

shat karma: six purification practices for the inner and outer body; part of the hatha yoga system

shaucha: cleanliness; one of the five niyamas

Shiva: God as the destroyer, as the element of change and transformation

shri chakra: an energy center within the sahasrara chakra complex, in the crown region of the head

shubhechha: virtuous desire; first of seven stages in spiritual practice

shunya: the void, beyond subject and object; also called loka lok

siddha: perfected one; highly advanced yogi; one who has attained high powers

siddhis: supernatural powers

so–ham: subtle level of the mantra "ham-sah"

Sri Isha Upanishad: a description of the Lord of the world; upanishads are philosophical treatises attached at the end of the *Vedas*

stambha: stunned; stiffness; one of the eight purifying emotions

subtle body: one of three "bodies," represented in the macrocosm and microcosm, which is composed of seventeen energies; sometimes called astral body

sumeru: top; the center of sahasrara chakra; also called mula prakriti

sushumna nadi: the main subtle nerve channel, located in the spine

svadhishthana chakra: energy center in the spine, at the level of the pubic bone

svadhyaya: self-study; one of the five niyamas

svarbhanga: cracking of voice; one of the eight purifying emotions

sveda: sweating; one of the eight purifying emotions

tamas guna: one of three essential qualities; quality of resistance, inertia, destruction

tamasic: anglicized adjective of tamas guna

tanmatras: the five subtle elements; the subtle objects of the subtle senses—sound, touch, light, flavor, odor

tantra: system of spiritual discipline that teaches through sublimation of emotions; a method of worship using mantras and mandalas; a method of healing by exciting the emotions

tantra yoga: spiritual path of transcending the senses

tantric: anglicized adjective of tantra

tanumanasa: one-pointed mind; third of seven stages in spiritual practice

tapas: austerity; self-discipline; one of the five niyamas

tattva: element, of which there are five: earth, water, fire, air, and ether

treta yuga: the second of four yugas; age of three-quarters truth

turyaga: complete isolation; immersion in God; last of seven stages in spiritual practice

ujjayi pranayama: breathing technique in which the air is inhaled through partially closed glottis, somewhat like sobbing

vairagya: dispassion

vichara: self-inquiry by asking, "Who am I?"

vicharana: reflection; second of seven stages in spiritual practice

vikara: impediments which keep a being in bondage—existence, birth, change, decay, and destruction

vijñana: knowledge of the world; scientific knowledge of the elements

visarga: aspirate sound in Sanskrit

Vishnu: God as the preserver

vritti: thought wave

vyana prana: one of five primary life forces (vital airs), which spreads throughout the body and four fingers' width around the body, creating the aura

yama: restraints; the first limb of ashtanga yoga

yantra: instrument; a diagram composed of geometric forms and colors; a method of healing using diagrams, herbs, and medicines

yoga: lit. "union"; path of spiritual disciplines for attaining enlightenment

Yoga Vasishtha: Hindu treatise on methods of yoga

Yogananda: a spiritual teacher and yogi who lived from 1893 to 1955; author of *Autobiography of a Yogi*

yogic: anglicized adjective of yoga

yuga: cosmic age; each creation consists of four yugas

SRI RAMA PUBLISHING

Other Books by Baba Hari Dass:

Ashtanga Yoga Primer
Cat & Sparrow
A Child's Garden of Yoga
Essays 1—Binding Thoughts & Liberation
Essays 2—Mind is Our World
Essays 3—Selfless Service: The Spirit of Karma Yoga
Fire Without Fuel
Hairakhan Baba—Known, Unknown
The Magic Gem—A Story-Coloring Book
Mystic Monkey
The Path to Enlightenment is Not a Highway
Sweeper to Saint—Stories of Holy India
Vinaya Chalisa (Forty Prayers)
The Yellow Book

For free catalog of our books and music please write:
Sri Rama Publishing, Box 2550, Santa Cruz, California 95063

SRI RAMA PUBLISHING

Music by Sri Rama Publishing:

Anjali—Melodies of Ancient India
Guru Purnima Songs
Horizons—Improvisations for Harp & Flute
Inner Light—Improvisations on East Indian Melodies
Jai Govinda!
Jai Ma Kirtan—Songs to the Divine Mother
Jai Shiva!—Kirtan for Shivaratri
Jaya Shambho!
Murali Krishna
Songs of the Ramayana
Sri Ram Kirtan—Volumes I & II
Tender Mercies—Hanuman Fellowship Women's Choir

For free catalog of our books and music please write:
Sri Rama Publishing, Box 2550, Santa Cruz, California 95063

MOUNT MADONNA CENTER

Mount Madonna Center, sister organization to Sri Rama Publishing, is a spiritual community and conference center inspired by Baba Hari Dass and sponsored by the Hanuman Fellowship—a group whose talents and interests are unified by the common practice of Ashtanga Yoga. The Center offers seminars throughout the year, including an Ashtanga Yoga Teacher Training course, several four-day Yoga retreats, a program of Yoga, Service, and Community, and many other programs in myriad pathways of spiritual growth. Located on 355 mountaintop acres of redwood forest and grassland overlooking Monterey Bay, the Center provides a supportive community atmosphere for relaxation, reflection, and a wide variety of learning experiences. Program participants are invited to join in all ongoing activities— celebration, work, and play. For information or brochure write: Mount Madonna Center, 445 Summit Road, Watsonville, California 95076.

SALT SPRING CENTRE

Another of our related communities, located on Salt Spring Island off Canada's beautiful west coast, offers a wide variety of programs—including in-depth Yoga retreats, self-improvement workshops, women's weekends, and healing seminars. Facilities may be rented for seminars, workshops, or gatherings. Participants enjoy delicious organic vegetarian meals, which inspired their cookbook, *Salt Spring Island Cooking,* currently a Canadian best-seller. For more information write: Salt Spring Centre, 355 Blackburn Road, Salt Spring Island, B.C., Canada V8K 2B8.

ASHTANGA YOGA FELLOWSHIP

Annual Ashtanga Yoga retreats with Baba Hari Dass, on-going Ashtanga Yoga classes, and weekly gatherings for inspirational study and devotional music (satsang) are held in Toronto, Canada. For more information please write: Ashtanga Yoga Fellowship, c/o Shakti Baird, 6479 The 2nd Concession, RR#3, Stouffville, Ontario, Canada L4A 7X4.

SHRI RAM ORPHANAGE

Author Baba Hari Dass receives no money from the sale of his books; his publications are dedicated instead to the needy and homeless children of India. In 1984, in a small village near the Himalayan foothills, he founded Shri Ram Orphanage—with the hope of providing at least some of these children with a better life. At first there were only two children, but within a year thirteen had come; then the earthquake in 1991 brought nineteen more, and we suddenly became a very large family. The last few years have seen wonderful changes there, as we started our own bilingual school with a current enrollment of 150 students; it serves our children as well as those of neighboring villages. We also built a larger kitchen, and constructed a large two-story dormitory building to accommodate the growing needs. The children of the Orphanage, several of whom came to us as infants with otherwise little chance to live, are now happy and healthy—laughing and running around in the new playground. At present writing (1997), plans are underway for a much-needed separate school building. With the support and help of many friends and donors, we feel fortunate to be able to make this small but significant difference. For more information about the Orphanage project please feel free to write to us.